Restoring Your Walk
with
God

Rodney Kingstone

Sovereign World

Sovereign World Ltd.
PO Box 17
Chichester PO20 6YB
England

ISBN 1 85240 037 4

Printed in Great Britain by
Richard Clay Ltd, Bungay, Suffolk

Typeset by CRB Typesetting Services, Ely, Cambs.

Dedication

To my wife Pat, for all the years of unselfish loyalty she has lovingly given to me, sometimes at personal cost to herself. To Amanda and Nathan our children who are a constant source of happiness. The best kids in the world.

Acknowledgements

Many have been the people who have contributed to my growth in the Christian life. To all those I say thank you. The following people have had a special effect upon me and occupy a special place in my heart:

The original members of the Pioneer Team who know all about me and love me just the same.

Norman Barnes, my friend who knows God.

Ross Paterson, who helped my dream come true.

Jackie Pullinger, my friend who always reveals Jesus to me.

Gerald Coates, for his friendship and sharpening of my mind.

Campbell McAlpine and the late Denis Clark, whose lives and ministries created in me the desire to go on knowing God.

Finally my fellow Elders and the members of Broadwater Christian Fellowship, for their love and understanding and keeping me on my toes.

Contents

Foreword

'"... we speak of what we know and we testify to what we have seen ..." Jesus Christ'　　　　　(John 3:11)

Jesus spoke through his knowledge of his Father. He spoke only that which had been revealed by his Father.

I have had the privilege of knowing Rodney since his first visit to Hong Kong three years ago and of this I am sure: he will only speak of what he knows and write of what he has seen. That is why I longed to read this book – it had to be the result of a personal search and of revelation. It could not only suggest a walk that Rodney is not prepared to walk himself. My prayer is that God uses this material and testimony to inspire many more of us to renew our walk with God and to enjoy Him.

Jackie Pullinger
Hong Kong
August 1989

Introduction

There is no greater subject on earth, no greater quest, than that of knowing God. This is the theme of this book, a continuous daily searching after God. Men and women throughout history, who have made an impact for the Kingdom of God, have been those who have had that heart thirst expressed by Paul, *'that I might know HIM.'* The prophet Daniel also knew that this was the key, *'the people who know their God shall be strong, and carry out great exploits.'*

The greatest need of the hour is for a people, a Church, with a holy pursuit in the knowledge of God, as God, as Father, as Friend. God, in all the Majesty of His glory, the perfection of His character manifested in so many ways, and especially through His beloved Son, Jesus, who said, *'he who has seen Me has seen the Father.'*

The author emphasises the need of a disciplined devotional life to enable the knowledge of God to increase, the knowledge that we are loved by God; that we cannot earn His love, but that in the knowledge of Him we will increase in our love for Him, and say with Peter, *'whom having not seen, ye love.'* The more we know

Him, the more we love Him, and the more we love Him, the greater is the capacity to worship Him. A right devotional approach will eliminate wrong concepts of God, and lead into a closer, intimate relationship.

I have known Rodney for thirty four years, first meeting him soon after he came to a knowledge of God, through Jesus Christ at a Billy Graham relay. All these years I have seen in him a desire to know God and be a man of God. This book is not merely theory, but comes out of a life which practises what he preaches. He with his wife Pat have been, and are, encouraging many, to be numbered among those who are on intimate terms with the Almighty.

Campbell Mc Alpine
July 1989

Chapter 1

Stopping the Decline

Walking across a hot dusty concrete camp in Hong Kong I was not expecting to hear God speak to me, so His voice came as somewhat of a shock. More than that, I was offended by the question that He asked 'Do you love Me or do you love the Kingdom?'. 'Surely it is beyond dispute that I love you, you know I do,' I replied. With this strong affirmation I expected the question to go from my mind but it continued to linger uncomfortably. Even the fact that I was in Hong Kong leading a team working with Jackie Pullinger in her ministry there did not lessen the question's insistence. As I thought upon it further, fresh questions arose in my mind. Why is it I spend more time planning projects for the Kingdom that I spend with the King? Why do I speak to leaders more about structuring the Church than I do about Jesus? Why is it in leaders' meetings I frequently attend around the country often the least mentioned name in conversation is Jesus? At this point the words of a magazine article came like a peel of thunder into my thinking: Busyness in the King's business is no excuse for neglecting the King.

1

Now I knew the original question to me was right and I knew what my answer must be. I had allowed the demands of leading a growing Fellowship, being part of a national team, speaking at conferences and meetings and taking teams abroad, to erode the time I spent personally with the Lord. By my actions and life-style I was showing a greater love for the Kingdom and its service than I was for the King himself.

It was time for my devotional life to be restored.

To begin any work of restoration it is important to understand what brings about the original decline. This is especially true for those who recognise that their devotional life has somehow been reduced to bare minimum, if not non-existence. It is also equally important for those who are enduring rather than enjoying their devotional life.

If we can understand why we are as we are, then when we have restored that area we will have eliminated the need for recurring restoration and can move forward to developing our devotional life.

What do we mean by the term 'Devotional Life'? As one reads through the scriptures the overriding message that leaps from the lives of those featured in them is simply 'They knew God'.

He spoke to them, they conversed with Him. They were intimately aware of His presence in all situations and places.

They were very personally acquainted.

This was far more than an acknowledgement of truth. It was more than a decision to believe which was solely intellectual.

It was even more than a cold decision of the will to accept that God was there. Here was a warm, intimate, comfortable, living experience of the living God.

A devotional life is this same intimate awareness of

the presence of God at all times that comes from specific times spent in His conscious presence, listening to Him, speaking to Him, and pouring out our worship to Him. Simply put, a devotional life is the time we give, and the attitude we adopt to really knowing and loving God.

Now there is a world of difference between knowing about God and actually knowing God.

We can know about the Queen or the Prime Minister without ever knowing either of them. Similarly we can know about God, Father, Son, and Holy Spirit, and still not know Him. We are then like the Israelites of whom it is said in Psalm 103:7 (paraphrase mine) 'They knew God's acts but Moses knew God's ways.' We can see what God has done or what He is doing but what a joy it is and what a privilege there is in knowing how and why He is doing it. To share the heart of God is real devotion and that takes time.

So what is it that brings about the decline of a devotional life?

Having a wrong view of God

There is a progression to paralysis that begins the moment we have a wrong view or understanding of God. This progression is clearly seen in the parable of the talents in Matthew 25:14–30. In verses 24 and 25 (Living Bible) we see that the wrong view 'I knew you were a hard man' led to the wrong emotion 'I was afraid' which in turn resulted in nothing being done 'I hid your talent, here it is back again'.

Too many believers approach their devotional time with a wrong view of God. Here are some of the more prevalent ones.

He disapproves of me

My friend Gerald Coates often says it is impossible to live under constant disapproval.

It is also true to say it is impossible to enjoy a devotional life if we think the object of our devotion disapproves of us. Now we probably do not consciously or rationally believe God disapproves of us but too often our speech or behaviour reveal that this is how we see the relationship. Consider these examples.

You have once again fallen to the same sin as last time and now you feel you just cannot come to the Lord to ask His forgiveness yet again. Last time was bad enough but to have done it again must surely have caused Him to give up on you. Now the result of this will be one of three courses of action.

1. We will not come into His presence

This is not because we do not want to repent but because we are afraid to confess the same sin again as we are unsure of His reaction to us.

We feel that He must be very angry with us or at best thoroughly disillusioned about us. When this happens Satan has scored a major victory over us as he has successfully kept us from coming in confession and repentance to God. Now the course is set for a decline in the time we spend with the Lord. To overcome this we must re-adjust our thinking. The truth is that we are accepted in the Lord Jesus (Ephesians 1:6). When we are in Christ we are acceptable to the Father and are also accepted by the Father. His forgiveness is unfathomable. We cannot possibly exhaust it and He makes it freely available to us. It is not our repentance that causes God to change His mind towards us and forgive us, but rather that our repentance causes us to be able to receive the forgiveness that God already extends towards us.

Our failure and sin must not keep us from the presence of God. We must make our failure and sin the reason for coming again and again to Him in order that we might receive His grace and forgiveness. This will in turn rob Satan of any ongoing victory in our lives.

2. We start promising God all kinds of things

Usually the things we promise most are increased deeds of service which we, wrongly, feel will get us back in His good books!

When we feel the need to keep placating the Lord the anticipation of enjoying our time with Him ceases to exist. Further trouble is added to this state of mind as we fail to keep the promises we have already made in the past. Consequently in our thinking God's disapproval of us grows even greater.

This kind of thinking ruins our devotion because we either do not understand the doctrine of the grace of God, or we have an inbuilt reluctance to accept His grace (unmerited and undeserved favour, as the Amplified New Testament says) as the grounds of all His dealings with us.

We must not adopt the attitude dealt with in Romans 6 which thinks that it does not matter if I keep on sinning, God has plenty of grace available. It is imperative, however, to understand that if we sin His grace abounds towards me and is totally sufficient for me. God does not want my promises but He does want my obedient response. Part of that response is to 'Come boldly unto the throne of grace, that we may obtain mercy, and find grace to help in time of need' Hebrews 4:16 (AV). The word BOLDLY here means without fear, unreserved utterance. Even our failures can be the launch pad to establishing a devotional life.

3. We live in the past

As we come to speak with the Lord we spend all of that time with Him repeating how sorry we are, how bad we are, and what failures we are.

To do this may appear to some to be very spiritual and very humble, but in the end we will not want to establish a devotional life that merely reinforces the fact that what God expects and what we are continually grows wider apart.

There has to come a time when we accept our forgiveness and celebrate the fact. We must put the full stop in on our past and begin to take action again. There was a point in Joshua's life when God told him to stop lying on his face upon the ground relating Israel's failure in battle and to get up and take action against the sin that had caused their defeat (Joshua 7:10).

Moses even caused the Lord to be angry with him, when he kept on protesting that he was a poor speaker and therefore unsuitable for the task set before him (Exodus 4:15).

It is of course right to acknowledge before God that without Him we can do nothing, but to keep on doing this instead of believing that through Him we can do all things is downright unbelief.

The same is also true when we are forever confessing that we are miserable failing sinners instead of affirming that we are now sons and daughters of God.

Another wrong view of God is:

He saved me to increase His workforce

This view has arisen because the Church has been taught for decades that 'We have been saved to serve'. This presupposes that God is only interested in me as a means to an end. We are simply pawns in a cosmic purpose. As long as I am being useful or making myself available to be used then God will respond to me.

We believe that God is short-staffed, so He saved us in order that He might be able to complete His work. I cannot emphasise strongly enough that we are not primarily saved to serve but we are saved in order to have a love relationship with God. He desires our company for its own sake. He still longs to walk and have fellowship with humans as He once did with Adam and Eve. It is out of gratitude for this wonderful relationship that we should want to serve Him through our service to others.

All devotion and love for God will inevitably suffer if we see Him as our employer or managing director and not as He is, our Father. Paul says 'The love of Christ constrains us' (2 Corinthians 5:14) God does not coerce us or threaten us to serve but instead He constantly woos us. The realisation and experience of Christ's great love moves us to serve and respond to God.

If we believe that we are only part of a workforce then it is not long before we begin to suffer from false guilt. This arises through us hearing that we should witness more. Or being asked questions like 'How many people have you led to the Lord last year?' or 'What are you doing for World evangelisation?'.

'There is so much to do and I am doing so little' is the thinking we fall prey to. Then the guilt begins. Now guilt will destroy any relationship unless it is dealt with. This form of guilt will destroy our love relationship with God by causing us to start attempting to do more for God or by causing us to promise that we will try even harder in the future. Sometimes we feel that it is all too much for us and so we gradually lose interest. Usually however we end up doing more and more things for God and having less and less time to spend with Him simply for His sake.

I remember a Christian worker saying to me recently 'If you are not tired out then you are obviously not doing enough for the Lord'. What a terrible concept to have of the one who said, 'Come apart and rest awhile' (Mark 6:31 AV). The taskmasters were left behind in Egypt. Why try and make the Lord into one in our experiences? The foundation principles of the Christian life as spoken of in Hebrews 6 include 'repentance from dead works'. A dead work is anything that is devoid of the life of God. We can so easily end up doing all manner of works for God, but because the time we spend in actually listening and responding to Him is negligible many of those works will not be expressions of His life and hence dead.

Closely associated with this wrong view of God is another reason for the decline of our devotional life.

We care too much about needs

This may sound strange, even wrong at first, but let us stop and think about it.

In the society in which we live we are surrounded by people in need. Personal needs abound on every hand. In fact because we care about people and are not indifferent to them we want or feel obliged to respond in some way to try and meet those needs. There are always people to see, letters to write, sick friends to visit, services to be taken, meetings to attend, evangelism to be done and as the list grows so our time available to spend with the Lord diminishes.

We need to realise that Jesus was not need-centred or need-motivated but He was always meeting needs. His secret was that He was God-centred and God-motivated. He declared in John 5:19 'Truly truly I say unto you, the Son can do nothing of Himself, but what he sees the Father do; for what things soever He doeth these also doeth the Son likewise'. Jesus knew what His Father wanted to be done in any given situation and He would not allow Himself to be pressurised into action outside of that. Even His own mother's plea at the marriage in Cana was not in itself sufficient to make Jesus act (John 2). When Jesus singled out the one man at the Pool of Bethesda from the rest of the multitude of sick people there and healed him Jesus left the multitude still in their need. Surely the only safe conclusion we can draw from this record is that He knew what His Father wanted done at that time and did that and nothing else. The scripture record leaves the implications that arise from such an event unanswered and we would do well to stop short of our speculations as well.

The only way we can move from being need-centred to being God-centred is by maintaining a strong devotional life. For this will enable us to know what God wants and will deliver us from our formulas and keep us dependent upon Him. The problem of living according to a set of formulas to be put into operation in any given circumstance is that we depend upon the formula and do not live 'According to every word that keeps on proceeding from the mouth of God'. There is absolutely no substitute to knowing God and hearing Him. Especially is this true when we are assailed on every side by needs. If we try to meet every need we hear of or feel guilty that we cannot do something about so many we will have a physical or emotional breakdown or alternatively develop a hard and cynical attitude. God does not want us to burn out for Him; He wants us to burn on for Him. When Moses was in the desert looking after the sheep it was not the fact that he saw a bush on fire that attracted his attention. It was the fact that this bush being on fire was not consumed. Burnt out bushes were a common sight then as unfortunately burned-out Christians are to-day. However one that continued to burn on with the glory of God was something different. Judson Cornwall once said 'The problem with leaders is not burnout but lack of intake'. Real sustaining intake only comes out of our devotional time with God.

To crack up through the service of God brings no glory to Him and of course effectively stops us from being of any help to others. It may appeal to the unwholesome traits of a masochistic nature but the answer does not lie in indulging those traits. The answer lies in becoming more like Jesus and serving as He did.

The final reason for the decline of a devotional life is:

We are afraid to let God know how we really feel

It is amazing how many devotional times are spoilt because we try to have a theologically correct time with God instead of being our real selves with Him.

We may have had a particularly irritating and frustrating time with someone. They have really got under our skin and now we are mad, even fuming inside. We are still all churned up as we come into the presence of God. Now we know that we should not be feeling or reacting like this so as we begin to talk with the Lord we make sure the words we use are correct. We pretend that we really like the individual and really are longing for their best. We tell the Lord how good the terrible time we had with them was because it helped in the building of our character.

All the time inside we are feeling we really want to get our own back or hear of some minor mishap befalling them. After all they deserve it. God knows what we are

10

feeling and what is going on inside of us and no matter how correct our language or content it does not fool Him. We on the other hand suffer because no relationship can fully develop when one of the parties engages in pretence.

We need to tell God all about our wrong emotions. We must tell Him exactly how we feel, how we would like to lash out verbally or physically at the other person. When we do this we will offload our problems and be open and ready to hear God say 'I understand but you need to repent'. Having emptied ourselves of everything that we feel or think by telling Him as it is, we can then be filled again with His love, grace, and Holy Spirit. Nice correct words uttered by us because we are afraid to be ourselves cause us to end up in deception or neurosis. God gives us the right and privilege to be ourselves with Him but His love for us will not leave us in that state. Instead with our co-operation He will go to work on those areas of our lives that require change. Think of some of the people in scripture who were themselves before God. The reason they could be so was because they were secure in their relationship with Him.

David in the imprecatory Psalms says some pretty horrific things. He prays for dreadful evil to happen to people. Much has been written about these Psalms to try and harmonise what appears to be ungodly attitudes with a more Godly or Christ-like spirit. However is this not the simple truth? This is a record of David expressing himself to God at these particular times exactly as he is feeling. Have we not felt the same things towards others that he is expressing? The difference is this, we pretend we are more spiritual and holy than we really are and know ourselves to be.

After having been the constant companions of Jesus,

11

listening to His teaching, James and John still wanted to call down fire upon the Samaritans and asked Jesus if He would permit it. Jesus rebuked them for it but they were uninhibited in saying it to Him (Luke 9:54). They were not afraid to be themselves and to let it show and Jesus took the opportunity of teaching them something further through it.

God will never be angry with us for being ourselves with Him. In fact He will respect our honesty and use it to teach us more about ourselves and Himself.

To be our real selves before God will enhance our devotional time. Someone has said 'Being yourself with God will not cause God to become disillusioned with you, because He has never had any illusions about you in the first place'. We must release ourselves from the need to talk to God with every doctrinal i dotted and t crossed and start enjoying a natural conversation with Him.

We do not have fellowship with a text book but with a living person.

Once I was speaking in a prison and met one of the prisoners who had become a Christian while serving his sentence. He told me how he used to go into the prison chapel and sitting by the altar would start speaking aloud to God in his East end of London accent and language. One day the chaplain overheard him praying and asked the prisoner if he would like the chaplain to teach him how to pray 'properly'. The prisoner replied that as God always answered every one of his prayers he did not feel he was doing too badly as he was. Do not try to impress God with your words or knowledge, for He will always look upon your heart.

The believer's devotional life should be a time and an experience that is looked forward to with joyful anticipation. It is the time when we can enjoy the intimacy of our

12

relationship with God. It is the time for really knowing Him and in knowing Him to discover just how wonderful He is.

Chapter 2

Sons Before Servants

When Jesus taught His disciples about prayer in Matthew 6:6–13, he told them to address God as Father. They were the opening words of what has become known as the Lord's Prayer. 'Our Father, who art in heaven'. Two years later when the disciples ask Jesus to teach them to pray He repeats exactly the same words 'When you pray, say, Our Father' (Luke 11:2 Amplified Bible).

Obviously Jesus is underlining the importance of beginning our prayers with a true understanding of our relationship to God. We do need to know that He is our Father.

I remember an occasion in my full-time ministry when I came to the place of embracing the fatherhood of God. Until that time I viewed God as some sort of supreme universal judge. He wanted to judge me and punish me for every misdemeanour that I made. Fortunately for me, however, Jesus stood inbetween me and God and held God back from getting at me. I knew and loved Jesus and I knew and experienced the Holy Spirit, but I was afraid and apprehensive about God the Father.

At this time my wife and I had adopted our daughter. She was only a few months old, and I was thinking about how I would tell her about her adoption. My mind started to think about how God has adopted us into His family and how He has given to us the Spirit of adoption so that we can cry "Daddy" to Him (Romans 8:15). I thought of how much I loved my daughter, of how much I wanted to care and provide for her, how she now had a right to our family name and how in time our possessions would belong to her. As I thought like this I realised that that was exactly how God viewed and loved me. He was not my judge, He was my Father. So powerful was the realisation that I knelt down and said 'From now on I receive you and embrace you as my Father. Oh what love, what wonder that you, the almighty, allow me to cry 'Daddy' to you'.

The fatherhood of God must be more to us than a formal acknowledgement of a truth or doctrine. It must captivate our hearts and our minds.

The devotional life cannot be built or based upon anything less than this. God desires us to be delighting in our sonship before we delight in our servanthood. He wants sons before servants. This is clearly seen in the parable of the prodigal son (Luke 15:11–32). The wayward younger son has returned to his father having both wasted his life and his possessions on sinful living. His father is so overjoyed at his son's return, that although the son was going to request his father to treat him as a hired servant, his father invests him with all the marks of sonship and openly displays his love and affection for him.

In response to the son's acknowledgement that he is not worthy to be called a son the father calls for a ring to be put upon his finger. This ring was probably a seal which would be used in transacting business and carried authority with it. It marked him as a member of the

15

family who could use the family name in doing business. Sons alone would have this honour, not servants.

Then the father called for shoes to be brought for his son. To be barefoot was the plight of captives (Isaiah 20:2) and also a sign of mourning (2 Samuel 15:30). In this action the father is signifying the son's restoration to liberty and that his mourning is over and joy is to begin. That is exactly what happens as orders are given for the fatted calf to be killed and a wonderful party to be held in honour of the returned son. This son has not served his father at all well but the father still acknowledged him to be his son. In verse 24 he says 'this my son'. With the party in full swing the elder brother returns from work in his father's fields and on hearing all the noise enquires as to what it all means. Learning that his brother has returned home and this is his welcome home party, the elder brother is furious and refuses to attend. His father comes out to him and begs him to join them.

The reply of the elder brother is most illuminating for it reveals his thinking and his inner attitudes towards his father and his work in verse 29. They are:

Service deserves a reward

'All these years I have served you yet you never gave me a kid' (verse 29 paraphrase mine).

Of course servants expect something in return for their work and it is so easy to begin thinking that we deserve something for our sacrifice, hardship, faithfulness, that we have experienced in our service for God. The elder brother has endured faithful service but he has not enjoyed fulfilling sonship.

Sonship lifts us above the realm of expected reward and fulfils us in the knowledge that we are always with our father and everything he has is available to us.

16

Keith Green's song 'O Lord you're beautiful' expresses it well in the lines 'And when I'm doing well help me to never seek a crown, for my reward is giving glory to you'.*

Many faithful servants of God who have been obedient in everything the Lord has said concerning His acts of service are hiding within themselves an unrewarded mentality. That is, I deserve something better than this.

It is often when we are tired that these thoughts and feelings make themselves known to us, and we must then be careful not to ascribe such thoughts to overdoing it but to the real cause of undernourishing our devotional life.

Servants become proud of their achievements, sons like to be proud of their fathers. Servants carry out the will of their masters without bearing their master's likeness. A son bears the likeness of his father and desires to be obedient to him.

One of the newer worship songs ends with 'I will boast in knowing you'. This is the true success of sons. Thank God for large churches, great offerings, many miracles, and full diaries, but none of these things merit boasting about.

Knowing Him, calling attention to Him, speaking of Him, and promoting Him because He alone is worth it, that is what is worth telling the whole world about.

Do not serve God for gain or give up serving Him if gain does not come your way. This was the issue raised and answered many centuries ago in the book of Job. Satan's basic premise was this: 'Job serves God only because of what Job gets out of it'.

God knew differently. He knew Job served Him because He was worth it. This question still has to be answered by us individually. 'Will you serve Him because He is worth serving or because you will get something out of it?' If you really know Him as your Father the resounding answer will be HE IS WORTH MY LIFE FOREVER!

Father is utilitarian

'You never gave me a kid that I might make merry with my friends' (verse 29).

What lies behind these words is the misunderstanding that the father only gives to his son that which is useful, not pleasurable.

Jesus frequently likened His Father to the image of a human father in His teaching. God the Father is infinitely more than an earthly father but he cannot be less so. Consequently when Jesus speaks of his Father's desire to give to us good gifts he illustrates it with the way earthly fathers treat their children. Could anything be worse to imagine than a father who only ever gave or provided things that proved useful for accomplishing a task and never gave anything simply for its own enjoyment or value?

Whilst it is paramount that we do not become self-centred in our praying, it is also true that we must never be afraid to make our desires and wishes known to God, and even request that He would give them to us. The same one who has given to us all things that pertain to righteousness and godliness is also the one who gives to us all things richly to enjoy (1 Timothy 6:17 Paraphrase mine).

There are some believers around who feel guilty about simply enjoying themselves. A young believer once said to me after he had returned from having a meal with some friends, 'I really enjoyed myself tonight. Oh, I should not have said that should I? I should have been looking for ways to have served God there.'

Servants by definition are always concerned about doing, but sons are concerned with being. As we understand more of the character of our heavenly Father we know He is not a utilitarian. Consider the many hues of green there are in creation or the fact that every individual snowflake is different in its pattern. The more we appreciate our position as sons the more we will appreciate creation and the enjoyment of living because these are the marks of our Father. It was Shakespeare who spoke of not having within this life of care the time just to stand and stare, and if we cannot as Christians take time just to enjoy our surroundings and discover in them the goodness of God, then we are poor indeed.

If you appreciate your sonship you will want to enjoy the beauty of creation, art, the intricasies of science, the warmth of friendships, all for their own intrinsic value, because in all of these things we see something of the wonder of our Father expressed.

What a pity that those who are only servants in their understanding miss these joys in their continual search for opportunities and/or usefulness.

Servants alone can end up being very boring people, but sons, as Jesus himself demonstrated, are attractive to others in their wholesome enjoyment of life. After all it is our Father who gives us life and we should show our gratitude to Him by enjoying it.

You never gave

This was the accusation that the elder brother levelled at his father. An accusing spirit will destroy our devotional life or our devotional life will destroy an accusing spirit. The choice is ours.

It seems incredible that we who are sons and daughters of the living God should ever point an accusing finger at Him. Sadly however we know that it is sometimes true. The words 'Why God?' spoken not as a genuine question but as an accusation have passed the lips of many of God's servants. Underlying the accusing spirit is a lack of confidence in our Heavenly Father and our standing as sons. The one thing the elder brother should have learnt about his father was that his father is willing to give when asked. The younger brother asked for his inheritance ahead of time and although his father was not obliged to give it to him he nevertheless did.

The father had never given to the elder brother because he had never asked. 'You have not because you ask not' says James in his letter, chapter 4:2. John in his first letter informs us in chapter 5:14 that we have confidence in the Lord because He hears and grants our requests.

The day my children refrain from asking me for things will be a sad day in my life. This is not because I always give to them what they want, but because I want them to feel free and confident in me to at least ask. God our Father also desires that we have a growing confidence in Him to 'ask what you will'.

Even when the elder brother had finished his tirade the father's first word to him was 'son' (Luke 15:31). It is not without significance that the father openly acknowledged both boys in their failures as sons. God is never in any doubt about our standing in and before Him and He does not want us to be in any doubt either.

What a wonderful father's heart is revealed to the elder brother when the father says in verse 31: (paraphrase mine) 'Son you are always with me and everything I have belongs to you'. Andrew Murray called this God's promise of unceasing fellowship and unlimited partnership. Such a statement was not given to hired servants but to an undeserving son. This statement should for all time remove any accusing attitude from us for what richness of grace and kindness is revealed in it towards us.

Also contained in this remark of the father's are the two experiential qualities of sonship. Firstly knowing you are always in His presence and secondly that all He is, and all that He has, is available to you.

Now we know that God is everywhere present and that He has promised never to leave us or forsake us, but this is very different from being consciously aware of His presence at all times. Such an awareness only comes through the time we take to know Him. This wonderful awareness of His presence will transform accusation into acceptance and panic into confident trust.

There was an occasion when I was to attend a conference in South East London. Arriving early I found the conference organisers were not ready to receive the delegates so I decided to go for a walk. Being in a residential area I nearly suffered culture shock. It was so unlike my town on the South Coast of England. Buildings were run down and many had a depressed look about them. Graffiti covered any blank space on the walls and overflowing rubbish bins and sacks filled the gardens and alleyways. As I walked on feeling the sense of gloom and hopelessness that seemed to hang over the area I noticed a gang of youths standing on a street corner up ahead. Being the only other person in the street my imagination began to work overtime. I was certain they would mug me at best, or leave me in need of immediate hospitalisation at worse. I started looking for side roads that I could turn up before arriving at where the gang was standing but unfortunately there were none. I was now inwardly tense and afraid and planning how I could escape with the minimum of harm. As such feeling increased a voice suddenly said 'Son what are you up to? I am here with you.' Instantly I became aware of God's presence. He was indeed walking with me, He was in control. At this my back straightened, my shoulders set, and without fear or apprehension I walked past the youths without a second thought about them. I do not believe now that they had had any thoughts about harming me but my imagination had produced fear within. It was this internal fear that the conscious awareness of God's presence dispelled.

In Matthew 8:23–27 the disciples awaken Jesus in the midst of a terrible storm at sea. As he wakes up Jesus asks His disciples incredulously 'Why are you so afraid, you of little faith?'. We must remember that most of the disciples were experienced fishermen. So this must have been an exceptional storm, even for those parts, to have so terrified them. In fact the word used in verse 24 for tempest suggests that there was an earthquake in the sea bed! Even so Jesus still asks them why they are afraid. I am sure, at least in their minds, the disciples answered 'Is it not obvious why we are afraid? We are all about to drown'. But were they? Jesus was with them and He was at perfect peace. His rebuke of their little faith was not because they were failing to calm the storm but because they failed to trust him in the storm.

He was with them in it. 'You are always with me' the father had told the elder brother. 'Lo, I am with you always,' said Jesus. Let your devotional life turn these words from purely memorised statements into the conscious awareness of his presence.

When Jesus talks in the gospels of the quantity of faith it is always in relation to faith as a fruit of the Spirit. Such faith is a growing thing. When Jesus speaks of the quality of faith ie having the faith of God (Mark

11:24) it is in relation to faith as a gift of the Spirit. I may exercise faith for some miraculous intervention of God in my life as God himself grants me to move in the gift of the Spirit, but that is very different from growing confidence in God that is the fruit of the Spirit developed in my devotional life as I spend time coming to know Him more.

Then there is the second statement of the father to consider. Everything I have belongs to and is available to you. Ephesians 1:3 states He has already, past tense, blessed us with every spiritual blessing in Christ. Forgiveness, cleansing, empowering, spiritual gifts, healing, and provision are ours in Christ. The New Testament proclaims over and over again that God wants to say yes to our prayers. Affirmative answers are His normal response. Negative answers should be His exception. Almost every text in the New Testament that speaks of making requests to God in prayer state or imply that He will answer yes.

To continually pray and have God say no to our prayers most or all of the time is no better than not praying at all, for the resulting outcome is exactly the same – nothing.

Jesus gave us tremendous promises concerning prayer in that God would say yes to our requests (Matthew 6:6).

Here Jesus says that the result of seeking the Father in secret would be an 'open' reward. Now an open reward by definition must be something that can be seen. It is impossible to see nothing! The open reward must refer to some positive answer that is received from the Father and can be observed.

Matthew 7:11 (NIV) 'How much more will your Father in Heaven give good things to those who ask Him!'. Such language suggests that the Father is eagerly

23

wanting to give what the believer is making a request for. The Father's heart is to give, such is His essential nature as revealed in the sending of Jesus to atone for our sins.

Matthew 18:19, Now the individual believer is coupled with another of like mind. Indeed this is more than a mental agreement, it is a harmony of life and purpose that is envisaged. However the outcome of such unity in life and prayer is 'anything that they shall ask it shall be done for them by my Father which is in heaven.' Whether or not our experience of prayer agrees in practice with these statements it is clear that Jesus in His teaching encourages his disciples to expect God to answer prayers in the affirmative.

John 15:16 (AV), 'Whatsoever you shall ask of the Father in my name, He may give it you'. This promise is the result of our relationship with Jesus being one of unity and appreciation of our calling by him to share his life and his Father's will. Nevertheless the promise is still one hundred percent positive 'He may give it you'. We can only escape the clarity of these words by engaging in some mental or theological acrobats that make them say that saying no to our prayers is a real answer from God.

John 16:23–24 (AV) 'Truly, truly, I say unto you, whatsoever you shall ask the Father in my name, He will give it you. Hitherto you have asked nothing in my name: ask and you shall receive that your joy may be full'. There are not many joyful Christians around who put the source of that joy down to the fact that their prayers only elicit a 'no' answer from God!

In all the above verses the emphasis is upon asking or seeking our 'Father'. The stronger the relationship is to God as Father so the less intense will be the attitude when one makes requests of Him in prayer. Imagine one of your children approaching you like this: 'My dearest father. I know that you care about me and understand me, but I now find myself in great difficulties. Indeed I don't know how I shall be able to manage, but of course you understand that. Therefore I really beseech you that you will find it in your heart, provided you have no objections based on your greater knowledge of events, to give me a bit of extra pocket money this week. O, please, p l e a s e, Dad etc. etc.' Would anything be more unnatural both to child or father whose relationship was strong and secure? No, the child is far more likely to come and say 'Dad I need some more money this week. Is it possible for you to let me have some?' Now I am not suggesting that we treat God flippantly, but I am calling for a strong secure relationship with Him that gives us total confidence to ask without trying to blackmail Him into response with a lot of preacher's rhetoric. It is both unworthy and unnecessary, and I fear is engaged in by those whose devotional life is not based and rooted in the experiential knowledge of God's fatherhood.

In our capacity as sons we should always seek to know why God at times says no to our prayers. This should not be done with an aggressive or rebellious attitude but because as sons we are seeking to learn our Father's will and ways. Scripture gives us many reasons why God says 'no' instead of 'yes' to our prayers. The following reasons are not exhaustive, but we should allow them to search our hearts before we just write off a 'no' answer as the sovereign will of God.

Has He heard me?

Unfortunately it is not true that God always hears us. Psalm 66:18 says, 'If I regard iniquity in my heart, the Lord will not hear me'. To regard means to see, look at, behold. If I allow unconfessed sin to remain in my heart, then inspite of what I may believe to the contrary, the Lord will not hear me. Sons of God will never set out to deliberately hurt their heavenly Father, and sin always hurts God before it makes Him angry. To allow iniquity to remain in our lives creates a barrier between us and God. It is not until that barrier is removed that God will pay heed to our prayers.

Wrong motives

James says in his letter, 'We have not because we ask not, we ask and receive not because we ask amiss in order to indulge our selfish desires' (paraphrase mine (James 4:3). Our motives are very often a complex maze to sort out and I would not advocate that we become introspective and acutely analytical in trying to see whether or not we are completely pure and selfless in our motives. I believe that we know easily whenever we are being totally selfish and avaricious, and in those rarer times of uncertainty then the Spirit of God will let us know that what we are desiring does not have its roots in His life and desires within us. Maturing Sons become less and less concerned with their wants, and more and more concerned with God's desires and will.

Unforgiveness

In Mark 11:25–26 it appears that Jesus adds a strong qualification to his remarks on answered prayer recorded in verse 24. In that verse Jesus says 'What things soever you desire, when you pray, believe that you have (already) received them and you shall have them.' Then he immediately speaks of the need, when we are praying, forgiving anybody that we have anything against. If we will not forgive Jesus says then neither will our father forgive us. To the extent that we are forgiving, that is the extent to which we are like our heavenly Father. As sons of God we should bear His moral image and likeness. Our unforgiveness clouds that image in our lives, and consequently another barrier is built between us and the Lord which needs to be removed.

We must not only confess our sin to God but we must also grant as an act of our will our forgiveness to anybody who has wronged us.

Bad marriage relationships

Where there is disharmony in the home there is a hindrance to our prayers (1 Peter 3:7). In our home life, if we are the husband, then we are to represent Christ to our wives. That is, we ought to remind our wives of Jesus. If however we are the wife, then we are to represent the Church to our husbands. That is, we are to remind our husbands of the Church. Either way as sons/daughters of God we should manifest our father's characteristics to each other. In doing this we remove any hindrances that there may be to our receiving from God. For if our home and married life is truly reflecting the relationship of Jesus to his Church then we are truly coming into a unity both of the Spirit and of life which will result in spiritual authority when we combine together in prayer.

Unbelief

It is surely selfevident that if we want our prayers answered then we must believe that God will answer them. Jesus reminds us in Mark 11:22 (NIV) to 'have the faith of God'. Unbelief is unknown in the vocabulary of heaven, and totally unknown in the character of the

Trinity. Unfortunately it is all too prevalent in the lives of God's children. The mountains of adversity, difficulty, and resistance all too often remain in our lives simply because we can not, or do not, speak in faith to their removing. Sometimes we do not believe that anything will ever change. When God speaks it happens. His word is an event. We need to develop an attitude of constant expectancy in our lives. After all we are involved with the living, all prevailing God.

Expectancy is not itself faith, but it is difficult for faith to be released when there is no expectancy in our lives. The cripple at the Temple Gate when Peter and John went up to pray 'expected' to receive something from them Acts 3:5. Then he received and exercised faith in the name of Jesus to be healed (verse 16).

If we are living a devotional life in a negative attitude then we need to repent and begin to live expecting God to manifest and express himself to us in answered prayer.

Discouragement

Sometimes we do not receive an answer to our prayers simply because we give up praying before we should. It was Jesus again who said men ought always to pray and not faint. We need to learn perseverance in prayer. When I was in Hong Kong in 1986 I was privileged to meet and speak with David Wang of Asian Outreach. David told me how he had gone to the Phillipines to minister on healing. Soon after he arrived he was called to the hospital to pray for a little girl who, being brain damaged and with a severely enlarged heart, was on a life support machine. When he arrived at the hospital he found the parents holding the now dead child in their arms and the equipment being removed from the room.

Together with the parents and some brothers David prayed for four hours for the little girl to return to life. After four hours of praying, although there was no visible sign of life, those present had a quiet assurance that God had heard and answered their prayers. From that moment they stopped asking God for the girl's life, and began praising Him for granting it to them. A little while later the child began to breathe, suck her thumb and respond to her mother's touch. She was and is alive and well. Having told me this David then said, 'Rodney, the reason why so many Christians never receive an answer to their prayers is because they give up too soon. The only time you stop praying is when you either know you have been granted the answer, or else God tells you to stop'. How grateful we all are that the Lord continually perserveres with us and His Church. That is the reason that perseverance should be a quality of sonship.

Chapter 3

God wants Friends

One problem that frequently faces leaders is 'how to keep motivating their congregations'. Even if you are not in leadership the same problem applies. How can I keep myself motivated? The answer is the same in both situations – Jesus. As leaders we need to continually present Jesus to the people and as people we need to continually see Jesus. We cannot be moved to serve God in mission simply by hearing numerous statistics and seeing coloured slides. We cannot be motivated to live godly lives by learning only pragmatic principles. Ultimately we must see ourselves in relation to Jesus. To speak of, or call for sacrifice is pointless, unless we set it in the context of the sacrifice of Jesus. Evangelism, mission, and devotion inevitably find their meaning, expression, and challenge in Jesus. John Bedford said to me at a conference on Mission that his answer to leaders who frequently ask him how to keep their churches going is this – Preach and present Jesus to your congregation.

The disciples after all 'followed Jesus', not an eloquent description of what they would or should be doing with their futures.

If we are to motivate others and ourselves this way, then we must learn how to touch the heart of God, and be able and ready to receive as He unveils His heart to us. To share as it were God's secrets we need to become God's friends.

There is something very special about a genuine friendship that is not found in any other relationship. You can be a child but not respond to your parents. Indeed parents may not share their plans with you simply because you are their child. In the last chapter we emphasized the need to enjoy our sonship. Now we move on to enjoy the privilege of sharing friendship with God.

The word 'friend' in scripture means 'dear to, loved'. It implies warmth, intimacy and trust. It is these qualities that God looks for in us. When we have them towards God they will express themselves in the following ways.

Consistency

Proverbs 17:17 (NIV) 'A friend loves at all times'.

How easy it is to be happy and to serve God energetically when everything appears to be going well for us. How strongly we feel we will always walk in obedience to God when positive blessing abounds. Alas, how different it is when our prayers seem to be ignored, or we receive only negative answers, when our vision dies and the sense of accomplishment is replaced by frustration and despair. It is however in these latter times and experiences that friends of God still love Him and constantly affirm that love. The circumstances make no difference to our love for God. This after all is the way God loves us. No matter what we do, or say, or become, He loves us at all times. To love God at all times does not depend upon nice feelings but upon a decision of

31

the will. We must choose to love Him. When life and circumstances are no longer harmonious and easy then we must decide to love still. The moment we decide to do that which is right, when we decide to align ourselves with the truth, the Holy Spirit gives to us his enablement to carry out our decision. That is why we must never confuse the choice of our will with simple willpower. The decision to choose lies with us, but the power to do lies with Him. When God therefore commands us to love Him with all our hearts we can. He is constantly at work in our lives to turn our aspiration into His achievement. To be a friend of God we must decide to love Him at all times and in all circumstances.

Loyalty

Proverbs 18:24 (NIV) 'a friend who sticks closer than a brother'.

Friends of God do not attempt to systematise Him so that when He does something new they miss it. Whenever we believe that God must work in a certain way and no other, we show our ignorance of Him. This is true also when we believe that He must work only with one particular doctrinal group.

Friends of God do not walk with a set of ethics or even principles, they walk in harmony with God. They stay close to Him, eager to go where He goes, and to be involved with what He is doing. There is no way you can remain close to God except by developing your devotional life. Jesus spoke of being yoked to Himself in Matthew 11:29. When ploughing with a yoke of oxen there would be a lead ox that the other one would follow. Bob Mumford amusingly applies the metaphor like this. If you are yoked to the lead ox and he wants to rest if you try to go on you will end up with very sore shoulders. If however you want to rest when the lead ox wants to move on you will end up with very sore ears. Now if the lead ox wants to turn left or right, and you try to go straight on you can expect a very painful neck! We must stick close to Jesus. Many is the time when we are so busy getting things done that we are unaware that Jesus is wanting us to rest for a while with Him. Friends of His that are sticking close to Him will know when that time is.

At other times we are reluctant to move on with God or to step out upon His promise. Fear, apprehension, self-indulgence or even plain laziness hold us back. Friends of God will always want to be moving in the direction and at the time that God is moving Himself. It is the mark of the overcomers that they follow the Lamb wherever He goes (Revelation 14:4). Surely it is no coincidence that these words were written by the best friend of Jesus, the apostle John, the same one that literally stuck close to Jesus by leaning upon his breast at the last supper.

Intimacy

Song of Solomon 5:16 – here the bride says of the bridegroom 'This is my beloved, and this is my friend'. Intimacy with God is a privilege open to every believer, but it is not automatic. It begins as a strong desire in our hearts, and continues all through our lives. The Apostle Paul expresses it in Philippians 3:10 'that I might know Him...'. This cry from the Apostle's heart was not uttered shortly after his conversion. It was his cry and longing some three years before his death. How glibly at times we speak of 'knowing the Lord' as if conversion gives us full knowledge of him. Friends of God are satisfied only by the ongoing revelation of Himself to them. This is not the knowing of knowledge but the knowing of experience. In the heart and mind of a true friend of God lies an insatiable thirst to know God intimately. One of the older choruses had a line that said 'To know Him is to love Him'. This is a wonderful as opposed to a vicious circle. The more we love Him, the more we will want to know Him. The more we discover of Him, the more we will want to love Him. This cycle of knowledge and love will never be broken in the life of the friends of God.

If God is wanting friends then how can we become one? In the Old Testament the designation 'Friend of God' is reserved for two people only, Abraham and Moses. (2 Chronicles 20:7 and Exodus 33:11 respectively). When Jesus comes in the New Testament the designation 'friend' is widened to a group ie the disciples. Friendship with God is not reserved for a special few. It is open to all true disciples of Jesus. The privilege can be ours if we will respond, and the consequence of such friendship will be that God constantly shares His heart openly with us. This sharing of God's heart was the characteristic of Abraham, Moses and the disciples.

God said of Abraham 'shall I hide from Abraham that which I intend to do?' (Genesis 18:17) (paraphrase mine). This was prior to the destruction of Sodom and Gomorrah. Such a revealing of the heart of God was designed to inspire a response of intercession from Abraham. God does not share with us simply to increase our knowledge. He shares with us in order that we might co-operate with Him in bringing about His purposes.

When Abraham stood ready to sacrifice Isaac upon the altar as God had instructed him (Genesis 22), did Abraham only see a substitute ram? No, he saw more than an animal. The veil of time parted and he saw God's ultimate and only source of salvation, 'The Lamb slain before the foundation of the world'. Jesus said in

34

John's gospel chapter 8:56 'Your father Abraham rejoiced to see my day: he saw it and was glad'. Abraham called the place 'Jehovah-Jireh' which also means 'In the mount of the Lord it shall be seen'.

He most certainly saw more than the literal surroundings on that occasion. He shared the heart of God.

Moses, we know, knew the heart and mind of God. The psalmist says Moses 'knew God's ways'. Moses not only knew the blueprint of the Tabernacle God wanted made, he knew what the heavenly tabernacle was like as well. He knew the substance behind the shadow and could interpret the tabernacle accordingly. He had been shown it by God Himself.

The disciples had had revealed to them by Jesus those things that God the Father had told Jesus. John 15:15 'I no longer call you slaves, for a master doesn't confide in his slaves, now you are my friends proved by the fact that I have told you everything the Father told me' (Living Bible). Even when it came to revealing future plans for God's redeemed community and the world, Jesus showed them to His friend John (Revelation 1:1–2).

In the lives of Abraham, Moses, and the disciples there are truths revealed which, if we follow, will lead us into becoming friends of God.

Abraham

In James 2:23 it is clear that friendship with God occurred when Abraham responded in faith to God's word. Faith is always a response to God. Far more important than trying somehow to get faith is the need to hear God. 'Faith comes by hearing'. When we hear then faith comes. It responds to His word and His voice. Anything else is only hope or optimism. Responding to the word of God was a characteristic that marked Abraham's life. It began with his initial call of God in Ur of the Chaldeas (Genesis 12:1) but it never ended there. We also need to be continually responding to the word that God speaks to us and, in order to hear it, we must have times of listening. Each response that Abraham made called for faith and obedience, and sacrifice was always involved. Sacrifice is the measuring rod by which God determines the reality of our love for Him and our faith in Him. 'Greater love has no man than this, that he lay down his life for his friends' (John 15:13 NIV). Responding to God will mean laying down our lives for our great Friend. Thus, when God first calls Abraham, the sacrifice that Abraham has to make is to go against the tide or status quo. At the time Abraham was called to leave Ur and travel west the movement of the nations was eastward. That is the opposite direction so Abraham's move appears illogical at the time. To make matters worse imagine Abraham having to tell his idol worshipping community that the God who was giving him instructions was invisible, and not even represented by any form of carving! Abraham's reputation is fast going down, but he has heard God. Centuries later another will come who also 'made himself of no reputation' and made the supreme sacrifice, constantly going against the tide. For us to take a stand against popular yet unbiblical thinking, immorality, religiosity, injustice etc. will cost us something, but we will be God's friends. There are in Genesis three other things that occurred before the point is reached where Abraham is called God's friend.

Abraham is not materialistic

In the story recorded for us in Genesis 14 Abraham had the opportunity to become even more wealthy that he already was.

The King of Sodom, grateful that Abraham had gone after armies that had defeated him, and had conquered them and brought back the people and possessions that had been taken from Sodom, made Abraham an offer. It was this. Abraham need only return the people to the King of Sodom, all the possessions Abraham could keep for himself. Enormous wealth was staring Abraham in the face, but he refused saying 'I will not take from you a thread even to a shoe latchet, and I will not take anything that is yours, lest you should say, I have made Abraham rich' (Genesis 14:23).

The essence of materialism is not what you've got, but what has got you. Abraham had and owned a lot, but none of it had a hold on or owned Abraham. This is why in Genesis 15:1 God said (paraphrase mine) 'Abraham, I am your exceeding great reward'. The materialistic attitude will keep us from ever moving towards being one of God's friends. It manifests itself when we want more personal gain. When we put more energy into receiving blessings instead of knowing the blesser. God will entrust with more those who are unconcerned about personal increase, and will call those His friends who will spend more time knowing Him than laying up treasure for themselves. Of course by definition and implication one cannot be devoted to God and devoted to materialism at the same time. One or the other will take first place, as Jesus said 'You cannot serve God and riches'.

Abraham cares more about commitment than comfort (Genesis 14:14)

When Abraham heard about the defeat of the King of Sodom by the four kings and their armies and how in the fighting Lot, Abraham's nephew, had been taken prisoner he decided to do something about it. He armed his servants and set off after the victors. There was danger involved. There was no guarantee that Abraham would return, or if he did, that he would be unscathed. However he was committed to his nephew. Lot was family.

Such a committment towards God and one another is required of us in our Christian lives. As the Father, Son, and Holy Spirit are committed to us in bringing us into maturity and securing our destiny, we must express our devotion to God by our commitment to one another's growth, and development in God.

It is clear from the story that Abraham took a risk in going after the warring kings. Those who would be God's friends will likewise take risks for God. I do not mean that they will live and act irresponsibly. I mean they will always be prepared to leave their safe areas and be stretched in their loving and serving God. Anyone can trust God sitting in an armchair dreaming of exploits for Him. God calls us into 'risky' situations to be doing something for Him. It is this unconcern for personal safety and comfort which Abraham exhibited that caused God to say to him 'I am your shield' (Genesis 15:1 NIV).

When King David's men risked their lives to get water from the well at Bethlehem for David to drink, it was because they had been close to David and had heard him sigh his desire. They were committed and devoted to David. We will not worry about risking our lives for Jesus if we are living close to him and hearing his desires and wishes for us.

Abraham believes for the impossible (Genesis 15:6)

After Abraham had returned to the King of Sodom the people and possessions which had been taken in battle, when he refused the riches the King of Sodom offered

38

him, then God appeared to him in a vision and promised Abraham a great reward. Abraham's reply was 'What will you give me, seeing I have no child?' (verse 2 paraphrase mine). This is Abraham's great desire to have his own son and heir. He and his wife Sarah are now getting on in years and are unable to have a child due to their old age. God's response is that Abraham will have seed as numerous as the stars in heaven. Upon hearing this, Abraham believes God, and it is counted unto him as righteousness. The years then proceed to roll by with no sign of the promise coming true until it is physically impossible for Sarah to conceive. In all that time though Abraham continues to believe what God has said to him.

Friends of God simply believe what God has said. The devotional life causes us to hear what He is saying and our faith in that must remain firm at all times. We are all prone to believe for the possible or even probable, but how difficult it sometimes becomes to believe for the impossible and improbable.

Whether we believe or not largely depends on how well we know the person making the statement. It will depend on how trustworthy we know their character to be. That is where friendship comes in. It is impossible to truly believe unless you have heard God say it and are convinced that He is completely worthy of your trust. It is the devotional life that ensures that these things are really true in our lives. If you are a friend of God you will know when He speaks to you and that those words will be true in any circumstance or situation that seems contrary.

Like Abraham we need to 'Stagger not at the promises of God through unbelief ... being fully persuaded that what He had promised, He was able also to perform' (Romans 4:20–21).

Moses

A tragic incident in the history of Israel is recorded in Exodus 33. Israel has been delivered from the pursuing Egyptians by the miraculous passage through the Red Sea. They have travelled on through the wilderness witnessing the miracles of care and provision. Eventually they arrive at Sinai where Moses is called up the mountain to meet with God. They witness the awesome power and glory of God upon the mountain. They even hear His voice. Now the hours turn into days and the days turn into weeks and there is no sign of Moses's return. In his absence the people request Aaaron to make them gods and soon they produce the Golden Calf idol which they begin to worship. As a result of this God sends Moses back down the mountain and judgement is executed upon the idolaters. There is however another consequence of this idolatry, which is referred to in Exodus 33. Up until this time there had stood in the centre of the Israeli camp a special tent called the tent of meeting. It was here that the Lord would come and meet with Moses and the tent signified the presence of God in the midst of His people. As a result of the idolatry the tent of meeting was now removed from the centre of the camp and pitched outside the camp. According to the rabbis this was about four fifths of a mile away. God was thus signifying that sin always removes Him from the centre of our corporate or individual lives. Sin will alienate us from God and rob us of the awareness of His presence. Sin and Jesus can never have the central place in our lives at the same time.

This is another reason why the devotional life is so important. It helps to ensure that nothing replaces the centrality of Jesus in our lives. The most effective way of dealing with sin is to 'see' Jesus. Isaiah found that when he saw the Lord he became aware and appalled at his own condition of uncleaness (Isaiah 6). The writer to the Hebrews in chapter 12 tells us to lay aside the sin that so easily besets us by looking unto Jesus. I know of no other way to 'see' Him than by developing a consistent devotional life.

Moses is determined

Now that Moses has to walk nearly a mile to reach the tent of meeting he has to be determined to make the journey. He does not find the time to make it, he has to make the time to do it. The majority of believers never find the time for a devotional life, they have to make the time for one. This is another mark of being a friend of God. We must put ourselves out in order to be one. Another aspect of this journey to the tent of meeting was that Moses would be seen to be making it by the people as he walked through the camp. What did they think about him? Was he admired or criticised? Was he held in esteem or laughed at behind his back? Whatever may have been the answers it did not matter to Moses. He was determined to meet with God. There will be times when we are misunderstood, our motives questioned, and our use of time a topic of gossip when it is known that we are putting ourselves out to meet with God. It is this determination that will in the end lead us into becoming one of God's friends. It is not a legalistic or compulsive determination, but one born of a longing to be in His presence with no other distractions.

Moses knows friendship does not come easily

The history of Moses's life prior to the announcement that God spoke with him face to face as a man speaks to his friend is one of hardship. He cannot be brought up by his own parents. He chooses to identify with the suffering Hebrews rather than enjoy his position as a prince of Egypt. He has to flee as a fugitive from Egypt, leaving behind his adoptive mother, friends, colleagues and his own racial people. He who had been groomed for rulership now finds himself in the wilderness looking after a flock of sheep and he does not even own them. Forty long years pass by until one day he encounters God. The burning bush episode changes his life. He then returns to Egypt to deliver the Hebrew people. It is not an easy task. He is not listened to at first, and when eventually he leads them forth he begins another forty year period of being on the receiving end of the peoples' moaning, grumbling, and criticism.

There is abroad an idea in the minds of Christians that our experience should be one of power, praise, victory, provision, health and healing without any suffering or pain at all.

Even the devotional life is portrayed as a quick easy pray with a bit of thanks thrown in and endless personal blessing the result. This is a travesty of the gospel. I firmly believe and practice prayer, praise, victory etc. but I also know that if we want to reign with Him we must also suffer with Him. Moses needed to be aware of God at all times. To regularly meet and hear from Him was fashioned upon the anvil of difficulty. Do not resist the unpleasant dealings of God in your life; they can be your launch pad to devotion. Do not give up when things appear to go wrong or become worse. This is exactly the time you need to be drawing near to Him. In fact need and difficulty can send us to God quicker than anything else. So why not be grateful for them instead of grumbling about them? Those difficulties can be turned into the causes that make your friendship with God possible.

The Disciples

Jesus, in John 15, summed up everything we have been saying regarding friendship with God. He told his disciples both the result of such friendship and the condition for such friendship. The result in verse 15 is 'Jesus confides in his friends and reveals the Father to them'.

The condition is obedience. The scripture says 'To obey is better than sacrifice' 1 Samuel 15:22. I believe it is also true that instant obedience is better than delayed obedience. The story has been told how at the Keswick convention some years ago, a young man came down for breakfast in his hotel and found himself sitting with an older well-known man of God. The message of the night before had been powerful in its challenge and the young man had gone to his room wrestling with an issue of obedience. Anxious now to impress the older man he said 'I wrestled with God all night, but finally I surrendered at 4 a.m. this morning'. Without lifting his eyes from his breakfast the old man replied, 'Pity you did not do it earlier and had a good night's sleep'. God will always win in the end but His friends will seek to obey sooner rather than later. Such obedience is needed to the words of scripture as well as to those personal words that God speaks to us. In both cases we need to know what He has said and what He is saying and for that we need our devotional time.

Chapter 4

Distinctive through Devotion

In all our service for God, irrespective of how it is expressed or manifested, we need to be distinctive.

Our service must be more than the spiritual counterpart of a charity or other aid organisation. We must have a distinctive mark.

This distinction is not a matter of being evangelical and/or charismatic. It is not brought about because we hold to any particular doctrinal position. We are to be distinctive by the manifestation of the presence of God with us.

We may have the right message and correct content and still not have an awareness of the presence or life of God, in the message or the messenger. The same is true of our approach to scripture. Scripture is full of the revelation of God, for it is the revelation of God. It speaks the truth of God, has the doctrines of God, and yet we can read it, memorise it, and even study it without having an encounter with the living Christ. The written word of God should lead us to the living word of God, Jesus. When we are not encountering him through and in the scriptures we are in danger of becoming professionals of the book instead of revealers of his glory.

We need to be distinctive so that when we are serving and ministering to others they are aware of a quality in that service and ministry which is a manifestation of the presence of God.

The New English Bible translates Exodus 33:16 as 'How can it ever be known that I and thy people have found favour with thee, except by thy going with us? So shall we be distinct, I and thy people, from all the peoples of the earth?' This knowledge that God is with us is not something that we have to convince others of. Instead they should know that it is true. It is the experience that the Apostle Paul speaks of in 1 Corinthians 14:24–25 where the unbelieving or unlearned, coming into a gathering where the spirit of prophecy is being released, confess themselves that 'God is here'. There is an awareness of the special presence of God.

We know that God is everywhere present. He is after all omnipresent. However when the tabernacle and the temple were built the presence of God was especially manifest in the Holy of Holies in the inner court. Between the cherubim on the ark was manifested the shekinah glory. Of course God was present everywhere else upon the planet and throughout the universe at that time, but it was the manifestation of His special presence that made Israel distinct.

The Old Testament priests who were the ministers of the people were also distinct. This came about through the smell of incense which had impregnated their skin, hair and clothing as they spent time ministering unto the Lord in the inner court. The incense itself was distinct. No duplication of it was allowed. You could not make it, buy it, or use it for yourself. It was only for use in the inner court.

Service to and on behalf of the people took place in the outer court of the Tabernacle. Service unto the Lord took place in the inner court. When the priests came to serve men in the outer court, it was known whether or not they had spent time in the inner court by their smell. That aroma for us is none other than the life of Jesus expressed through us. It is his character being reproduced in us by the working of the Holy Spirit. It does not happen automatically but is brought about by and in the times of our devotional life. Many Christians, leaders and others, are serving men in the outer court without spending time serving God in the inner court. The result of this activity is human wisdom, and counsel based upon previous experience instead of the word of the Lord. It leads to mechanical or professional answers devoid of compassion and empathy. It is seen in quick prayers, clichés, and 'let's get home quick' attitudes instead of ministering the life of God to the people. You can serve men without serving God but when you are serving God in your devotions you will be distinctly serving men. Jesus reminds us in Matthew 5:13 how easy it is to lose our distinctiveness. 'You are the salt of the earth; but if the salt have lost his savour, wherewith shall it be salted? It is thenceforth good for nothing, but to be cast out, and to be trodden under foot of men'. Here Jesus expresses the loss of distinctiveness as becoming tasteless. The words mean to become tasteless through foolishness. The result of this loss is to be trampled under the feet of men. In Revelation 11:1–2 the same phrase 'to be trampled under foot' is used.

In these verses the rod symbolises protection. The people who are therefore enjoying the protection of God are those who are in the inner court. Those who are in the outer court alone are the ones who are trampled under foot. Could anything be more clear? Distinctiveness and protection are gained through the time we spend in the special presence of God. It is foolishness to believe that we can carry on effectively ministering to others without spending time ministering to the Lord and being ministered to by Him. Sadly too many are trying to, inspite of their knowledge to the contrary. We will sing of being in His presence, talk about being in His presence, read about and preach the need of it, but we must do it. The world needs to see the glory of God. Ours is the privilege and the responsibility of being the means to show them. This will only happen as we 'With open face beholding as in a mirror the glory of the Lord are being changed from one degree of glory to another even as by the Lord who is the Spirit' (2 Corinthians 3:18).

The place to behold His glory is in the inner court of devotion. It is here that we become like Him for what we worship we become like. Then we outwork and express Him in the outer court of our service to others.

Of all the prophets of the Old Testament Ezekiel speaks the most about the inner court. He has some salient lessons for us in our day.

Divine Illumination or Human Reason

In Ezekiel chapter 8 we have a tragic scene portrayed. Ezekiel is transported in the Spirit to Jerusalem. He is brought to the very threshold of the inner court of the Temple. The angel who accompanied him now proceeds to show Ezekiel a series of sinful happenings that have polluted the Temple and the worship of Jehovah. Before Ezekiel sees these events the angel informs him that each one will be more detestable than the previous one. There will be a progression of evil.

The first scene Ezekiel witnesses is an idol of jealousy erected for worship in the Temple. Idolatry being practiced in the very place set apart for the worship of

God. Next he is shown the elders of Israel worshipping idols, unclean animals, pictures of all manner of crawling creatures. All this is being done in secret. Thirdly he is shown women weeping for the god Tammuz.

This Sumero-Akkadian god of vegetation, whose descent into the nether world signalled the seasonal fading of life, was also worshipped as Adonis and Aphrodite, who was connected with sexual immorality in the worship rites. The weeping was part of the ritual prior to the rite of the god being found and then sexual licence often occuring.

Each scene is obviously growing in its abomination until at last the angel tells Ezekiel that he will see the final culmination of evil (Ezekiel 8:16). Now this is what Ezekiel sees:

'And he brought me into the inner court of the Lord's house, and, behold, at the door of the temple of the Lord, between the porch and the altar, were about twenty five men, with their backs toward the temple of the Lord, and their faces toward the east; and they worshipped the sun towards the east'.

At first sight, this scene does not appear to be the final worst act of evil. Why is the worship of the sun by these twenty five men worse than all the evil that has preceeded it? It is because of what is represented here. The sun is the natural source of energy and light for the world. The Spirit of God is, however, the supernatural source of energy and light for the believer. The men in the scene have turned their backs on the source of divine energy and illumination which is found in the inner court. Instead they have substituted natural strength and reasoning to accomplish worship and the work of God.

How like them we are at times. We labour to the point of exhaustion in our own strength. Ceaseless activity is

48

heralded as the hallmark of success. We look to our organising ability, energy, enthusiam even natural giftedness to accomplish the work. Even so, corporately we still have not completed the task. Individually we sometimes look with despair at how little has been achieved by all our working and striving. Stop before it is too late for you. Go back not to the drawing board, but into the presence of God. In Ezekiel chapter 44:15– 18 the Lord tells Ezekiel that when the priests draw near to minister to the Lord in the inner court they must only wear linen clothes. They must not wear wool or anything that causes sweat. Sweat in Genesis 3 was a mark of self-effort brought about by the curse. We are not to minister unto the Lord with any sign of self-effort upon us. We have been redeemed from the necessity of using natural strength to accomplish God's work and will. We will accomplish it by the energising of the Spirit of God.

As Jesus neared the end of his life, the first place that his blood was shed was upon his brow when he sweat, as it were, drops of blood in the Garden of Gethsemane. He was redeeming us from the curse of self-effort. The same is true of purely natural reasoning. Leaders and churches have looked at techniques used by multinational companies for growing or administering and have concluded 'it works for them. Let us adopt it for our church'. We who should be turning the world upside down are in danger of letting the world turn us. We sit down with our committees, our formulas, even our questionnaires, and look for answers as we incessantly talk and discuss. We are forever seeking quick answers, strategies and ideas at the shrine of human reason.

Will we never learn to seek revelation, both personal and corporate, waiting before God? The well-known words of Zechariah (4:6 NIV) 'not by might, nor by power, but by my Spirit, says the Lord' do not primarily refer in their context to doing acts of power. The context is to give light and illumination to the temple of God. The Holy Spirit is the Spirit of revelation to the Church and to the believer. He waits to give us revelation and is, more often than not, kept waiting by us as we try everything else first. Even our past experiences of blessing and anointing are not to be relied upon as a substitute for present revelation. When the priests entered the inner court, the first task they did was to trim the wicks of the seven-branch lampstand. They had to cut off the charred portion of wick in order that the wick might burn and give off light. If the wick was not trimmed then it would only produce smoke, not light. If this happened, then the inner court would be in darkness, for there was no means of light other than the lampstand. The wicks became charred because they did the job for which they were designed. They had not done anything wrong. It is the same with us. As we engage in what we should be doing we need the Holy Spirit to remove our reliance upon past blessing and even past inspired methods. That is the charring. We need to receive present direction in order to burn on with nothing remaining in our lives which would hinder the fullest expression of the radiance of Jesus. Be thoroughly grateful for all that is past, but go on to seek him for all that is to come.

The Inner Court Incense

We said previously that the incense gave the priests their distinctive aroma. This aroma was symbolic of the life of Jesus. The Holy Spirit wants to work the character and life of Jesus in us in order that it may be seen through us. This work of the Spirit needs to take place in our devotional life. Such working of the Spirit may occur in a meeting, but we must not substitute the meeting for our consistent time of devotion. If we do, it is like rectifying those illnesses which could have been prevented by living and eating responsibly at home, by having to spend time in hospital.

The ingredients which went into the making of the incense reveal to us areas of the character of Jesus that we need in our lives. The incense was an equal compound of four spices. They were Stacte, Onycha, Galbanum, and Frankincense.

Stacte

This was a sweet spice which oozed from a tree (probably the storox) in drops. It was released sometimes by making an incision in the tree. All of this indicates the work of the cross in our lives. It is the sweetness which comes from pressure rather than blessing. Pressure will never produce sweetness all the time we are fighting for our rights or will. Sweetness of character will only come as a result of pressure when we have truly died to ourselves. As A.W. Tozer put it 'The glory and benefits of the cross can only be enjoyed when we know we have been crucified on it. We do not live stretched on it, but in the power of His resurrection. We cannot be raised until we have died and that is painful'. The extent to which we embrace the work of the cross in our lives will depend upon how much we have seen of the power of the cross in our devotional lives. How often in private do you pour out your gratitude for the work Jesus accomplished on the cross? How easily do you surrender to the painful process of sanctification in your life? To adequately express Jesus we must take up our cross. We must voluntarily embrace the hardship, discipline, and suffering which following him will always entail. This can be done with joy if we are meeting regularly with him who has already done it.

Onycha

If Stacte speaks to us of the work of the cross then Onycha speaks of the work of the Spirit. Onycha was the lid of a shell mollusk or the claw of a shell fish. When it was burnt it gave forth a sweet odour. The shell was hard, yet when burnt released fragrance. All of us have certain strengths in our make-up. If these are exhibited or used without being under the control of the Spirit then the observers or recipients of them will never recognise Jesus in us. The Holy Spirit wants to control all our strengths, touching them, as it were, with holy fire in order that the motives behind them may be pure and the exercise of them may be in the anointing of God.

We must also take care that in exercising our strengths we do not crush or threaten others. Instead we must release the fragrance of Christ which will inspire them to follow after him and also to draw near to him. The person who has not experienced the touch of the Spirit, the fire of Spirit, or the filling of the Spirit in private devotions is in danger of being a showman in public.

Galbanum

This spice came from two umbelliferous plants. That is, the plant had many stalks coming from one main stem. These stalks in turn were topped by a convex clutch of flowers.

Everything about this spice speaks of diversity in unity. There was one spice from two plants, one stem from which many others grew.

As we get to know God better through our devotional life so we will understand that He expresses Himself in a diversity of ways and people. The Apostle Paul says 'There are different kinds of gifts but the same Spirit. There are different ways of serving but the same Lord. God works in us and through us in differentways but it is still the same God' (1 Corinthians 12:4–6 paraphrase mine). The devotional life will prevent us from becoming stale or stereotyped. It will stop us from getting in a rut in our Christian experience. Our devotional time will create and also enhance our creativity. It will even help those who believe they are uncreative to become creative. God, who is the supreme creator and expression of creativity, will impart to us, albeit in finite measure, the ability to be creative in our worship and service if we will spend time with Him.

We will also be able to appreciate, honour and love those who do and see things differently from us. Not, I hasten to add, concerning the fundamentals of the faith. Our times of devotion should cause us to become tolerant of difference, but intolerant to sin.

Frankincense

Frankincense was the fragrant gum of a tree grown in India. It is white in colour and was regarded as a precious perfume on its own.

The Magi in Matthew 2 brought it as a gift to Jesus. In Revelation 8:3 it is offered with the prayers of the saints unto God.

It speaks of purity and preciousness, the very essence of the life of Jesus. According to Jesus in Matthew 5:8

(paraphrase mine): 'It is the pure in heart who shall see God'. William Barclay in his 'New Testament Wordbook' (SCM Press) says purity means 'those whose motives are absolutely unmixed, whose minds are utterly sincere, who are completely and totally single-minded'. Could such an examination of our lives be carried out, except in the presence of the Lord? Can such quality of life be ours except the Holy Spirit applies to our hearts the righteousness of Jesus? Purity of heart does not come by effort, but by obedience and repentance in the presence of the Lord. Then we see God. This is not only reserved for us at death or his coming but we can 'see' him in our lives and living here and now.

When we learn to minister in the inner court we will begin to realise that the presence of God brings certain benefits to us. We do not give Him time in order to gain benefits, but because He is worth our time. However such is His nature that benefits will accrue to those who spend time in His special presence. The following benefits await all those who will make such a time a priority in their lives.

Rest

'My presence (literally my face) shall go with you and I will give you rest' (Exodus 33:14). The 'rest' referred to is not the rest that comes from a life of ease. It is the rest that follows after a victory has been won in battle. It is the period between conflicts cf.Deuteronomy 3:20. Those who know how to live in the presence of God are assured of victory. This of course is our ultimate destiny when the kingdoms of this world have become the kingdom of our God and of His Christ. In the meantime we are called to wage spiritual warfare. 'For we wrestle not against flesh and blood, but against principalities, against powers, against the rulers of the darkness of this world, against spiritual wickedness in high places'. (Ephesians 6:12). The spiritual conflicts ahead which await all of us are going to be tough, but the battle is the Lord's. Therefore we need that time to be spent in His presence in order to be refreshed, receive battle plans and enjoy the victory that will be ours.

Renewal

'Glory and honour are in His presence, strength and gladness are in His place' (1 Chronicles 16:27). Isaiah reminds us in chapter 40:31 that 'those who wait upon the Lord shall renew their strength...' The word renew here means to change. In the presence of the Lord is the place to exchange our weaknesses for His strength and our weariness for His refreshment. This change rarely happens in a split second. It takes time to come into effect. The change effected in us is directly proportional to the time spent with Him. To expect to be renewed in strength, vision, and ministry by spending as little time with God as possible is like a person expecting to recover from major surgery by drinking a bucket full of glucose instead of being put on a drip.

Strength is not the only thing that is renewed in His presence. Gladness is as well. The Psalmist says 'In thy presence is fulness of joy' (Psalm 16:11). Weariness and pressure, criticism and failure, together with sorrow and other things, all cause a depletion of our joy. Once again the place of renewal is in His presence. Many have sung the following chorus again and again, and when they have put the words into practice have experientially discovered its truth:

I will enter His gates with thanksgiving in my heart,
I will enter His courts with praise.
I will say this is the day that the Lord hath made,
I will rejoice for He has made me glad.

Gladness is the result of the working of God in our lives, brought about and sometimes explained in the times spent in worship with Him.

Let us return regularly to the inner court that we may behold Him and go forth to serve Him, being distinctive by the expression of His presence that we manifest to others.

Chapter 5

Beholding His Glory

One of the saddest events in Israel's history was when the Glory of God finally departed from them. The Glory of God was and is the visible manifestation of God, or that which makes Him impressive. Israel had come into being as a nation and a kingdom in the presence of the Glory of God (Exodus 24:16–18). The Glory of God had been seen upon Mount Sinai by the whole nation. The Glory of God dwelt amongst them in the Holy of Holies of both the Tabernacle and the Temple.

Some of their outstanding leaders and prophets had seen it with their own eyes; Abraham, to whom the God of Glory appeared, and Moses, who had prayed 'Show me Thy glory', and had ended up with his face shining with it, Isaiah who beheld the Glory of God and received his prophetic calling as a result. These and others knew that you cannot behold the Glory of God and remain unchanged. Neither can you behold His glory and not affect the lives of others. Israel was supposed to be the container and revealer to the nations of the Glory of God.

They had even received the promise that one day God would fill the whole earth with His glory (Numbers 14:21–22). They no doubt believed that they would be used somehow to accomplish it. Their history, however, is well known for their fluctuation between obedience and rebellion, between righteousness and unrighteousness. The Glory of God came and went until finally it departed forever. The nation saw it no more. Their decline became permanent. Darkness settled over the earth. It is apparent from the account in Ezekiel 10 and 11 of the Glory of God departing that God was reluctant to remove His glory from them.

The Glory of God is seen hovering over the Temple, then it moves and hovers over the city, and then it moves from the city to the Mount of Olives and then accompanies the cherubim to heaven.

God does not lightly withdraw the manifestation of His Glory and presence from His people, but now Israel's light of life and witness has gone. Isaiah's prophecy of world evangelism through a declaration of the Glory of God now seems an impossible dream.

Even more impossible of fulfilment appears Isaiah's prophecy that world evangelism would result in all nations and tongues seeing God's Glory (Isaiah 66:18–19). The Glory had departed. Now the centuries roll by. Then one night an extraordinary event occurs.

Upon a Judean hillside some shepherds are looking after their sheep. It is like any other night in their lives. The sheep are safe, the fire burns, conversation is engaged in. Suddenly it is not like any other night at all.

The Angel of the Lord appears and 'the Glory of the Lord shone round about them' (Luke 2:9 AV). The Glory of God had returned.

This time though there would be a difference. The Glory of God would be seen in an individual – JESUS.

This extraordinary night heralded the birth of Jesus. The angels had to declare 'Glory to God in the highest', for Jesus was the 'brightness of the Father's Glory and the express image of the Father's person' (Hebrews 1:3 paraphrase mine).

The Glory of God is back among men and it can be seen. John the Baptist, at the beginning of his ministry, declares, quoting from Isaiah, 'The Glory of the Lord shall be revealed and all flesh shall see it together' (Luke 3:5 paraphrase mine). What John the Baptist says refers to Jesus. John the Apostle in chapter 1:14 of his gospel tells how the disciples 'Beheld His glory, the glory as of the only begotten of the Father'.

God had always desired to dwell among men in order to reveal His splendour to them and to manifest His splendour through them. In the Lord Jesus this was and is completely accomplished.

There was, however, something even more wonderful, or should we say remarkable, to come. It was this. Through the Lord Jesus the Glory of God would be in us and be seen through us! The Apostle Paul says, 'We all, with open face beholding as in a glass the glory of the Lord, are changed into the same image from glory to glory even as by the Spirit of the Lord' (2 Corinthians 3:18). The likes of you and I can behold His glory and be changed into it.

This is where our devotional life comes in. We cannot behold His glory and be changed into it unless we are acutely aware of Him. Many a person has looked up into a star-filled sky and simply seen only the stars, or perhaps has appreciated the beauty of creation. The person, however, who is aware of the presence and person of God will look up into the same night sky and see God's Glory (Psalm 19:1). It is in our devotional life that we should encounter the Glory of God.

Not only do we behold His glory but we contain it. The Glory of God is the treasure we have in earthen vessels referred to in 2 Corinthians 4:7. We must never begin to think that the vessel is the important factor or element in this. Nor must we seek to call attention to the vessel. The important factor and centre of attention must be the content of the vessel, that is, the Glory of God in us. To a thirsty man the plastic drinking cup only has relevance and importance in his life if it contains something to drink. It is the same with us as vessels of the Glory of God. How can we behold His Glory? How can we be changed into His Glory? How on earth can we manifest His Glory?

The answers to these questions are found in our devotional life.

It was during a devotional time in the life of Jesus that our ultimate destiny of being beholders and sharers of His Glory was both assured and revealed. In John's gospel chapter 17 verse 24 Jesus prayed these words 'Father I will that they also, whom thou hast given me, be with me where I am: that they may behold my Glory, which thou hast given me'. Whilst this verse speaks of our coming privilege of seeing him in all his Glory, verse 22 of the same chapter tells us that the Glory is already ours. 'The Glory which thou gavest me I have given them...'.

How then do we see and show it? In a word by worship.

A.W. Tozer said that worship was the missing jewel of the evangelical church. If that were true, then it is certainly true that worship is the missing jewel of personal devotion. Devotional times invariably consist of lists of prayer requests plus a Bible reading and that is all. It is not enough.

We will never behold the Glory of God until we break through into worship.

It is always true that what a person worships is what that person will become like. It is also true that we never worship anything to which we do not attach the highest value. Therefore we must see Jesus. In 2 Corinthians 4:6 (AV) the Apostle Paul says 'God who commanded the light to shine out of darkness, hath shined in our hearts, to give the light of the knowledge of the Glory of God in the face of Jesus Christ'.

We must remember that to see the Glory of God is God's gift to us. We can never merit it and we cannot simply produce it. God grants it to us in response to our desire and worship.

We must also further remember that in order to reflect His Glory we are totally dependent upon the work of the Spirit of God. It is He who changes us from one degree of glory to another, as we allow Him to work in our lives. We definitely cannot do this by using our determination or willpower. We can only surrender ourselves to the Spirit of God as He works in us. Such surrender to Him is in itself worship, as it is the bowing down of ourselves and our ability before Him. This needs to be a continuous attitude in our hearts, and at times a posture we adopt before Him. Every act of true worship that we engage in will contain for us some element of sacrifice. When, in Leviticus 9, the Glory of the Lord appeared to all the people, it followed the sin offering and burnt offering that Aaron made on behalf of himself and the people. The Glory of God in the life of the believer is a result of the sacrifice of Jesus made on our behalf. The ongoing experience of the Glory of God in our lives is a result of our sacrificial worship of him.

Imagine for a moment that you are now having a devotional time with the Lord. How are you to worship? Scripture is full of examples which contain important lessons for everyone in terms of our attitudes and actions.

61

One of the first times that the word worship is mentioned in the Old Testament is in Genesis 24:26. Here is the account of Abraham's servant being sent by Abraham to find a wife for Isaac. Eventually he arrives at a well and prays that the girl who first comes and offers to give him and his camels a drink will be the future wife for Isaac. Almost immediately Rebekah comes and fulfills the conditions of his prayer. Verse 26 (AV) records 'And the man (the servant) bowed down his head and worshipped the Lord'. This physical action of bowing the head is full of symbolic meaning. The head is the place of our intellect, thoughts and will. It contains our minds. Our mind, the ability to reason and make decisions, must be subservient to the Spirit. We are to love God with all of our minds but we are to worship in the Spirit. This does not mean that our worship is unreasonable or unintelligent, but it does mean that we are aware of the transcendent greatness of God. He is above our ability to totally comprehend, understand or contain. That is why we bow before Him, and yet in doing that we discover that He is within our ability to experience.

When Abraham's servant bowed his head in worship it was in response to the knowledge that God was in control of this circumstance and had answered his prayer. As we worship in our devotional life we need to remind ourselves that God is in control of all the circumstances of our lives. This includes all those which make no sense to us at all.

We need to recall His answers to our prayers and His leading in our lives and simply surrender (bow) all before Him. In such an act of worship invite the Holy Spirit to reveal to you the greatness of God. Ask the Holy Spirit to make you very aware of His presence. In the quietness surrender once more your self, your ministry, your talents and possessions and make all that you are and have available once more to Him.

Offer to Him your plans, and desires. Do not even pray about them for you are making Him, for His own worth and sake, the most important person, together with the worship of Him, the most important thing at this moment in your life.

Now you will begin to behold His Glory.

One of the reasons we have had so much trouble in seeing the Glory of God is because our vision has been taken up with so many other things. Consciously deciding not to concentrate on those things but to concentrate upon the Lord will enable us to 'see' Him. One song puts it like this:

'Just forget about yourself,
concentrate on Him, and worship Him'

Joshua at worship is another example we can learn from.

Verses 13–15 of Joshua chapter 5 record a meeting between Joshua and the Captain of the Host of the Lord. This person is none other than the Lord himself.

Joshua and Israel have at this time encamped in Gilgal in the plains of Jericho. They can see the city of Jericho standing as a blockade to their possession of the land of Canaan. The city is locked up, allowing no one to enter or leave.

One day Joshua was by himself near Jericho when he saw a man standing nearby holding a sword in his hand. Joshua immediately challenges him. 'Are you for us or for our enemies?' he asks. The man replies 'No, but as Captain of the Host of the Lord am I now come'. Instantly Joshua falls on his face on the earth and worships.

Joshua was not overwhelmed by this person's appearance but by the revelation that came with the words which the person spoke. Worship should always be the result when we hear the Lord speak to us. Worship should always occur when we receive a revelation of Jesus.

When the Lord spoke to Joshua his words did two things. Firstly they corrected Joshua, and secondly they revealed who the speaker was. Joshua had asked the question 'Are you on our side or our enemies' side?' The man had answered 'No, I am Captain'. He was telling Joshua that he was not going to respond to Joshua, instead Joshua must respond to him. Worship is not having God respond to us; it is always us responding to God. That is why we must develop our devotional life, so that we can listen, see, and respond to Jesus.

The Lord also communicated to Joshua the correct view of the situation. Joshua was on the Lord's side, not the reverse. How prone we are to constantly think that God is on our side as if we are the centre and God is there to do our bidding. No wonder with such an attitude our worship is often stunted, or non-existent. What a difference though when we constantly remind ourselves that we are on His side. He has chosen us. We are here to serve His purposes. He does not need us but He has chosen to involve us. When the truth of this hits us, then we will worship.

In reality you will never worship someone who only exists for your benefit. You will only worship someone for whose benefit you exist, and yet whom unreservedly gives Himself and continues to give of Himself for you.

'O come, let us worship and bow down:
let us kneel before the Lord our maker.
For He is our God;
    and we are the people of His pasture,
and the sheep of His hand.'

(Psalm 95:6–7)

When the Lord replied to Joshua 'As Captain of the Host of the Lord am I now come' he not only revealed who he was but he also showed that he was in charge. Had Joshua been speculating on how he would take Jericho? Was Joshua feeling the weight of responsibility to take the people into the Promised Land?

Whatever the answers may have been it was surely a great relief and assurancce to know the battle was not his but the Lord's. As we grapple with the problems of life and ministry what a relief it is to know that the ultimate responsibility lies with the Lord. Many have been the times, when being at the end of my tether, God has said 'It is alright. I am in control'.

In your devotional life do not see everything as being up to you, instead see God in his rightful place – in command and in charge.

As we follow the instructions He gives it is then that we see His glory. Joshua saw it when Jericho fell without a shot being fired. However, before he saw it he had previously lain prostrate on the ground before the Lord in worship. The Glory of God is not a mystical experience, it is the visible demonstration of His power. The visible demonstration is both the inspiration for our worship and also the result of our worship.

It is imperative that we learn to worship, and are familiar with worship, whilst we live here on the earth. If not we will not easily fit in with the routine of Heaven. In the glimpses of Heaven that we have in the book of Revelation scenes of worship occur five times. Worship is Heaven's normal activity. A.W. Tozer said 'I can safely say, on the authority of all that is revealed in the Word of God, that any man or woman on this earth who is bored and turned off by worship is not ready for Heaven'.*

---

* *Whatever happened to Worship?* Kingsway Publications.

One reason that Heaven is so taken up with worship is because God is clearly seen in all His glory. His power to accomplish His purposes is clearly seen. He is high and lifted up, creator, redeemer, His glory blazes forth and so worship occurs. This is our final destiny, but we can have a foretaste of it now. The Apostle Peter speaks of this final destiny in chapter 4:12–13 of his letter. Here, in these verses, is the ultimate revealing of Christ's Glory, and also a way for that Glory to be revealed now. Peter says 'But rejoice that you participate in the sufferings of Christ, so that you may be overjoyed when His glory is revealed' (NIV). Participation in the sufferings of Christ will result in His glory being revealed in us now. If we truly want to express and reflect his glory now then we must be prepared to suffer. Suffering and glory go together. The suffering that the Apostle Peter is speaking of is anything which tests our faith (Chapter 1:7, 4:12), or any form of persecution or rebuff that comes to us because we belong to Jesus (chapter 4:14,16).

The way to ensure that in these sufferings, and also through them, we see and express his Glory is to rejoice and be happy. Why should we and how can we, we may ask? The answer is in verse 14, 'For the Spirit of Glory and of God rests upon you', and 'on your part He is glorified'. To rejoice before God in worship will refresh the drooping spirit. It will turn a bitter and resentful attitude into a trusting and accepting one. It will turn our sorrows into an eternal weight of glory for us (2 Corinthians 4:17).

One of the most poignant acts of worship recorded in the Bible must be that of Abraham's offering up of his son Isaac.

The story is found in Genesis 22. Abraham, in response to God's command, sets out for the land of

Moriah. There he is to offer his only son Isaac, whom he dearly loves, as a burnt offering to the Lord. Abraham goes forth and after three days arrives at the appointed place. In verse 5 Abraham says to his servant who had come with him 'Abide ye here with the ass; and I and the lad will go yonder and worship, and come again to you'. Abraham links worship, faith and resurrection together. The act of sacrifice is his worship. His faith finds expression in the words 'We will come again to you'. This could only occur through resurrection and so Abraham became the first to anticipate resurrection life (c.f. Hebrews 11:19). These three elements need to be found in our acts of worship. It is in worship that we lay down all that we have and all that we are to God and Him alone. Worship is costly because it has cost the one we worship everything. Sacrifice once again becomes the measuring rod of the value we place upon the worth of Jesus to be worshipped by us. If we value Jesus so highly, why is it so difficult for us to sacrifice time in order to worship him?

Faith must also be present in our worship 'for he that cometh to God must believe that He is, and that He is a rewarder of them that diligently seek Him' (Hebrews 11:6). We need to believe that we will meet with God every time we come to worship. Anticipate it, expect it, and you will experience it. God's desire to meet with you and reveal himself to you is infinitely greater than your desire to meet with Him. From the act of creating man, God has always taken the initiative in meeting with us. It is God Himself who invites us to draw near to Him in order that He might draw near to us (James 4:8).

We should then move out from our worship time in the power of His resurrection. That worship and resurrection are linked together should be obvious, as we

worship one who was dead and now is alive forever-
more. Jesus also linked seeing the Glory of God with
resurrection (John chapter 11:40). True worship trans-
forms a credal statement 'I believe in the bodily resurrection of Jesus' into a living experience of his risen
presence. Worship both inspires and answers the heart
cry of the saints expressed by the Apostle Paul in Philippians 3:10 'That I might know him, and the power of his
resurrection'. As we surrender before him, believing
that we shall meet with him, and become impressed with
his presence, we receive his resurrection life and power.
This life of power will be shown in our morality, spir-
ituality and miraculous deeds. It is true that 'The people
who know their God shall be strong and do great things'
(Daniel 11:31 Living Bible). Where else other than in
worship in our devotional life can we ever really get to
know him intimately?

This story of Abraham and Isaac underlines again
that worship is the means for beholding His Glory.

Jesus, when in dispute with the Pharisees in John's
gospel chapter 8:56 (AV), said 'Your father Abraham
rejoiced to see my day: and he saw it, and was glad'.
When did Abraham see the day of Jesus? Surely it was
when Abraham, about to plunge his knife into the chest
of Isaac, was stopped by the Angel of the Lord and
looking around saw a substitute, a ram caught by its
horns in a thicket (Genesis 22:12–13).

At that moment Abraham the prophet gazed down
the corridors of time to a place called Calvary. There he
saw another substitute, a lamb called Jesus, this time a
substitute for the sins of the whole world, held not by a
thicket, or even by nails, but held to a Roman cross by
supreme love, dying in order that we might live. The
cross is the supreme, incomparable act of the Glory of
God.

Jesus did not speak in John's gospel chapter 17 of being crucified but of being glorified. Any sacrifice that we make in order to spend time in worship will always be completely overshadowed by the sacrifice of Jesus. Here we see suffering glorified, as it shows us the way to God is freely opened for us to take. We bow at the cross in order that we might worship at the throne. In both the cross and the throne we behold his glory and the Spirit of God begins to effect change in us, that will be felt by the world around us, that will enable the Church to be full of the manifest Glory of God. Such a Church will become the light of hope, life, peace, security and the light of salvation to the nations of earth.

'Arise, shine; for thy light is come, and the glory of the Lord is risen upon thee.

For, behold, the darkness shall cover the earth, and gross darkness the people: but the Lord shall arise upon thee, and his glory shall be seen upon thee. And the Gentiles shall come to thy light, and kings to the brightness of thy rising' (Isaiah 60:1–3).

For everyone's sake behold His Glory.

Chapter 6

Making Time and Making it Meaningful

One thing that can never be said about the Word of God is that it is unrealistic. The people of God in scripture faced the same kind of issues that we face. When it comes to the tensions arising from busyness they were no exceptions. In Acts chapter 6 we see tensions arising in the Church because of its growth. Those tensions threatened to erode the Apostles' times of devotion. This scenario can be repeated again and again in leaders lives of to-day. Indeed, in the world in which we all live it is not only a leader's problem. It affects us all.

It is strange how the very thing that helps promote growth and the blessing of God becomes threatened when growth and blessing increase. Our times of prayer can so easily be reduced because the growth such times have created now creates its own demands upon our time.

Many times we determine to set a time apart to be with God only to find the diary full of pressing appointments.

We must sort out our priorities and learn how to fulfil the other obligations. A closer look at Acts 6 will help us.

Be aware of your prime calling

The Apostles recognised the problem in the growing Church. They knew something must be done about it. The Greek widows had to be looked after and fed just as the Hebrew ones.

Now it might have seemed obvious that the Apostles should have offered to do the work themselves. After all there were twelve of them and only seven people were needed for the task. Perhaps even more important was the fact that they had heard Jesus' teaching on servant-hood first hand. 'He who would be great among you, let him be your minister and whosoever will be chief among you, let him be your servant' (Matthew 20:26, 27). Jesus had said of himself, in their presence, 'The son of man came not to be served but to serve' (Matthew 20:28).

The Apostles were not unwilling to serve tables but they knew their prime calling and priority. To give themselves to prayer and the ministry of the word was the priority. Likewise it must be ours also. We must firmly establish in our minds what our priority is and then work everything else around that. If you are in full-time leadership learn this lesson well and teach it to your people well. They do not pay you primarily to do a job but to buy you time to seek God. They must allow you time to be with God. That is your priority. We must put the emphasis in our lives that 'we are servants of God, not leaders of men'. Having established this priority we must now work it out in practice.

Delegate

We make difficulties for ourselves in arranging time because we fail to distinguish between the urgent and the important. Too often we are reacting to the urgent instead of planning the important. Of course sometimes the urgent and important are one and the same. We must however begin to correctly assess whether or not in any specific case they are.

In both cases something needs to be done but should it be done by us? The Apostles' answer to this in Acts 6 was delegation. Delegation will not only help us to plan time, it will release others into their ministry also. By becoming overbusy ourselves we actually hold back opportunities for others to serve. This can lead to their being frustrated because there is nothing for them to do.

To delegate can be difficult for some people. It is something we must learn to do. The work of God does not depend entirely upon you. He has a body consisting of people, all of whom have a place and part to play. Use them.

To help you in delegating tasks to others ask yourself the following questions:

What parts of your function can only be performed by you?

What parts of your function can be done by others?

What takes up the greatest amount of your time and makes you inflexible?

What parts of your function do you dislike most?

What kind of experience do others need in order to develop?

When we first set out to make time for our devotional life it will not be easy. All of a sudden we will remember all kinds of things that need to be done. We will find all kinds of demands being made upon us. 'How can I possibly find or make the time?' will be a pressing question. How can it be done?

Making time

The first step in making time for a devotional life begins

with your diary. Looking at any week will reveal a diversity of appointments already booked. Have you booked in an appointment with God? This single fact has been revolutionary to some. It will prove an enormous help to you if you write in your diary regular time with God. When people then ask if they can see you, or whether you can go somewhere etc. all you need say is 'sorry, I have a prior engagement'. If such a time with God is a priority do not feel it is the one appointment you can change or put off. God has a right to your time above that of anyone else. A simple diary entry can ensure that He gets it. Another thing about diaries is this. Do not take your diary to meetings. People often react immediately or emotionally at a meeting and then want to see you. If however they have time to think about whatever it was that caused such reaction, then a further meeting is often unnecessary. If like me you are a person who finds it very difficult to say no to people, then why not let someone else keep your diary for you? At one stage in my ministry I found this to be of immeasurable help when I directed all appointments through one of the ladies in the fellowship.

Step number two concerns the telephone. Some people cannot let a telephone ring without answering it. Others cannot concentrate even if they let it ring. Then there are those who are always concerned that it might be an emergency needing immediate attention. What are we to do? There are fortunately several remedies.

Buy an answering machine. These are now financially within the reach of all of us. The outgoing message can, if need be, have an alternative number to contact in case of absolute urgency. Even so you will be able to return the call probably within the hour at the latest.

Leave your house or office.

Walk or drive to a quiet place, sit in the car or by the

sea. Go into the country or even park. Consider using another church building that is open. If you are one of those who can ignore background noise then you might like to use the coffee lounge of a local hotel.

Inform others when you are unavailable.

This of course has the most benefit when such times are always the same. It creates the habit in others of knowing when to reach you and when not to try. Obviously you cannot inform every possible person who is likely to contact you. The main people I have in mind are those of your own congregation.

There is of course one other difficulty if you are having your time with God at home. That is the caller on the door step.

If there is someone else in the house with you then arrange in advance for them to open the door. They can say you are engaged at the moment and arrange another convenient time.

If you are there by yourself place a note on your door asking people to call back or phone back after a stated time.

To make time for God we must be disciplined. If we will stick to our intention then we will find that we have time available.

How then can we use such time? What do we do in that time?

It is important to remember that scripture does not lay down any rules for our devotional times. The following suggestions are made to give practical help and direction for a start. From this look to developing your own content and style of devotional time.

Off we go

The keyword for an enjoyable and profitable devotional

time is Relax. Do not try to make fervent intercession, receive profound insight and be overwhelmed by the presence of God in a few minutes. Take time to be at rest. Slow down and unwind. Remind yourself that the Lord is right there with you. Consciously realise that He is sitting in the chair next to or opposite you. If you are walking then be aware that He is walking alongside you. Say hello to Him. Tell Him about the surroundings, 'Lord, isn't that a great view?' 'Lord, I remember buying that ornament on holiday'. Let the conversation be natural and ordinary. Develop this conversational style with God all the time. I continually talk to the Lord when driving, shopping, playing etc. Over the years this has made me very conscious of His continued presence with me. Beginning this way of talking naturally with Him you will soon be very conscious of His presence. It is now the natural response to begin to praise Him. There are a variety of ways to do this. Choose from the following:

Begin speaking in tongues. Tongues are amongst other things a means of praise. On the day of Pentecost the crowds declared 'we hear them speak the wonderful works of God' (Acts 2:11 paraphrase mine). When speaking in an unknown tongue a person is principally addressing God, not man (1 Corinthians 14:2). With our spirit we are giving thanks to God, we are blessing Him.

Read aloud one of the praise Psalms. It is important to read the scripture aloud when we are on our own. It helps our concentration. It is more difficult for our minds to wander when we are reading aloud than when we read silently. It also has the benefit of our being able to hear what we are reading. It is amazing how hearing the words of scripture audibly inspires our heart to praise and worship the Lord. If we are reading the Psalm as an expression of praise to the Lord then I believe it should be audible, as praise in the scripture is always presented as audible and never silent. The following Psalms are particularly appropriate for reading: Psalms 66, 68, 92, 96–100, 107, 111–113, 145–150. In reading the Psalm watch for the stirring of the Holy Spirit within you. This occurs as He joins your desires to the words of the Psalm. For example Psalm 66:1–2. 'Make a joyful noise unto God, all ye lands: Sing forth the honour of His name: make His praise glorious'. As you read this you feel you want to express its truth too. So you say 'Lord I want to make a joyful noise unto you. Today my heart sings for joy for all that you have done for me. My sins are all forgiven. I have food, clothing and shelter. I will sing unto your name. Jehovah-Jireh you provide for me. You are faithful and you see and respond to my need, Hallelujah. I exalt you. May the peoples of earth give praise unto you'.

This will bring the awareness of the presence of God to you in a very real way. Let your heart and your spirit now give expression through spoken praise and thanksgiving. Praise is essentially declaring good and wonderful things about the Lord. Thanksgiving is saying thank you for what He has done for you. Spend some time in saying thank you. If need be make a list of some things you are grateful to God for.

All this has established in your experience that God, not you, is at the centre of your devotional time.

Now it is time to make your requests known to God. Ask Him for specific things.

Some people find it helpful to have a list and to record the date asked and the date when answered. In this way you have a record of answered prayer which acts as an inspiration to thankfulness. It can also act as a gauge to how effective our prayers over a period of time have been.

However you organise your petitioning of God it will help to have a plan. Acts 1:8 could be the basis for such a plan in your prayer time. Here Jesus spoke of Jerusalem, the disciples' immediate surroundings, Judea the area beyond that, Samaria spreading even further afield, and finally to the uttermost parts of the earth. We can begin by making requests for and on behalf of our family and ourselves. Next we can include our friends, church, leaders and our communities needs. Moving on we begin to pray for our nation, the government, moral and social issues in the land, the Church in the nation, education, family life and so on. Finally we come to the world. This is probably the most difficult part. There is however an excellent aid. I thoroughly recommend purchasing a copy of 'Operation World' by Patrick Johnstone.* This book features a different country each day of the year. It gives succinct information about the country and the needs for prayer.

Up until this moment you have done all the talking. It is now time to listen. After all God has something to say to you. Prayer is a two way conversation. Ask the Lord to speak to you now. Do not try to empty your mind or to make it go blank. Just sit quietly. Expect to hear His voice. Allow the Holy Spirit to direct your thinking and make a note of those things that come to mind. Do not be discouraged if at first you seem to receive little or nothing. Resist any attempt on your part to try and force God to speak to you. Listening is a skill which needs to be learnt.

During this time your Bible will be close by. The scripture being the revelation of God to us, we should therefore expect to see Him and hear Him through it. In order for this to happen we need to spend some time meditating in it. Take your Bible and decide which book you are going to meditate on. Leviticus and Chronicles

---

STL Books. WEC Publications.

are not the best books to begin with. Having decided which book to begin with or to carry on with, stay with that book. Do not keep switching from book to book or passage to passage. You need to hear God speak through the consistency of the book, for that is how it was written.

Before you begin to meditate you must rid yourself of wrong conceptions of meditation. Biblical meditation is not emptying the mind. It is filling the mind with the word of God. It is not trying to reach some heightened awareness of yourself. It is being aware of God speaking directly to you through the scripture. As used in the Bible the word 'meditate' means to ponder, muse, chew upon. So the important thing is not how much you read, but how meaningful what you have read is to you. That comes through pondering what has been written, chewing it over in your mind.

Let me give you an example. Suppose you are going to meditate on Luke chapter 5:1–11. First read the whole passage through. Then slowly read verse one thinking about it and imagining the scene which it speaks of. People are pushing and clamouring to hear the word of God. Now a question forms in my mind. Do I display the same sense of urgency to hear the word of God? This is God speaking to me and I must answer honestly. Perhaps the question is 'Why don't people surge around me or our church to hear the word of God?' As we think upon this God will give us insights about our situation.

Keep pondering the verse until no other thoughts are formed and it seems God has nothing else to say. Proceed to verse 2. Here it may be that you are struck by the words 'the fishermen were washing their nets'. You think 'dirty nets do not catch fish'. 'Am I a clean or dirty channel?' 'Do I prepare the means for catching men (evangelism) or just have a sporadic go?' Slowly verse by verse I become aware of God speaking to me.

78

Sometimes I may read several verses and nothing seems to speak to me. In such instances I do not try to get something but simply read on until I come to that which God wants to say to me.

The great advantage of meditating is you can continue pondering on a verse whilst driving, gardening or doing a multitude of tasks.

So far we have addressed ourselves to the content of a set-aside time of devotion. The following suggestions are not meant as an alternative to such a time but an addition.

The goal we are heading towards is the continuous awareness of God's presence and our response to Him. This cannot be achieved only by a set time. We need to develop a life of devotion throughout the spare moments of the day. For those engaged in full-time ministry or demanding jobs I can hear the objection 'We have no spare moments'.

Stop a moment and see if that is really the case. What about the time spent in travelling to and from work? What about the time spent in going to visit people? There are moments left after eating lunch and before returning to work. Most of us have more spare moments than we realise. The reason we do not utilise them for developing our devotional life is because we think such moments are too short. Alternatively we are not sure what to do in such a short time. These moments however small can be turned into profitable times. Remember, keep talking naturally to God. Just as it is helpful in our extended times with the Lord to have a pattern to base them on, so it is with these spare moments. The Lord's Prayer provides such a pattern for us. Taking it section by section we can pray it through in the spare moments of the day.

Begin 'Our Father who art in heaven, hallowed be thy

name'. Thank Him that He is your Father. Thank Him that you have been born again into His family. Thank Him for all the good gifts that He gives you as your Father. Scripture lists many of them including 'good gifts', 'the Holy Spirit', 'food and clothing', 'forgiveness'. Thank Him for the church you are joined to. He is not just your Father. He is our Father.

Now praise His name. Give thanks for all His covenant names mean to you. He is your Saviour, provider, righteousness, sanctifier, healer, shepherd, protector, peace. Pray for His name to be honoured in the land. Here you can mention a specific piece of legislation. You could pray for a specific situation and ask for God's name to be glorified in it or by it. In this way we can use each section of the Lord's Prayer as an inspiration to pray and praise. It also helps us in remembering where we left off when we come to resume in the next spare moment.

I am sure those of you reading this have a desire to develop your devotional life. Your desire alone however will not achieve the result. The difference between desire and achievement is discipline. We need to have a disciplined approach to our devotional time. I am indebted to David Matthews of Team Spirit for pointing out that the early Church had a disciplined hour of prayer. In the Jewish culture of New Testament times devout Jews prayed three times a day. They prayed at 9 a.m. 12 noon and at 3 p.m. In the Acts of the Apostles we find that the Holy Spirit came on the Day of Pentecost at 9 a.m., the hour of prayer (Acts 2:15). Peter and John went up to the Temple to pray at 3 p.m. (Acts 3:1). The result of that was the miracle of the healing of the lame man. It is clear from the first eight chapters of Acts that the early Church had regular, consistent times of prayer. They devoted themselves to it (Acts 2:24).

There is no by-passing the discipline in order to obtain the blessing. I have sought to show in this chapter that, however busy we are, we can still have and develop a devotional life.

I have asked two good friends of mine to write the following diaries of their devotional times. They had only two criteria to fulfil. Firstly they had to be very busy people. Secondly what they wrote had to be what they regularly practice in their devotions. It had to be real and honest.

The reason for this is to show that we can make time and to suggest ways in which to use it.

The first extract was written by an itinerant minister who also oversees a local church. He is a member of a national team of ministries and travels extensively in the third world speaking and encouraging national believers and missionaries.

The second contribution comes from a man who is involved in caring for a number of churches, travels to Scandinavia and is also an author and conference speaker.

The Diary of a Busy Itinerant Preacher

7.00 a.m.   Alarm One goes off.

7.01 a.m.   Alarm Two – the radio goes on, listen to four minutes of Radio London news – I never wake up, I emerge into the world.

7.02 a.m.   Switch on teamaker – hopeless without a cup of tea. Still emerging.

7.05 a.m.   Sufficiently awake to sip tea and read daily portion of the One Year Bible (NIV) Old Testament/New Testament, Psalm and Proverb.

7.25 a.m.   Move on to read Operation World by Patrick Johnstone – with my burden for the world this enable me to be informed and pray for every country of the world in one year.

7.35 a.m. Begin to pray. My usual order is:
1. Thanking the Lord.
2. Pray for the world and my many missionary friends.
3. My colleagues and fellowship.
4. My sick and needy friends.
5. My family.
6. My wife and myself.
7. Give thanks for another day to serve Him.

7.50 a.m. Finish – having drunk all my tea!
A shower and breakfast and at the desk between 8.30 a.m. and 8.45 a.m.

Diary number Two

6.45 a.m. Why do mornings always come so early? I don't feel led to pray today so I try to ignore the alarm. Then I remember the prayer meeting a long time ago when my friend Nigel earnestly sought God for victory over the bed clothes. 'There is no victory, you just get up' was the advice shouted across the room to him. I get up.

6.50 a.m. The kettle is on, the cat is fed and the coffee is beginning to filter. I take my wife a cup of tea, pour myself a mug of hot black coffee and head up the garden towards my office.

7.00 a.m. I find yet again that it is the little routines of life that prepare me to pray, rather than rushing straight in. That is especially true of the coffee! I open my Bible at the last place of reading. Alongside it I also open my 'One

Year Bible' and get some bread and wine ready for later. Now where is that devotional book I was reading?

7.10 a.m.   Now I am ready to start. So Lord where will we begin together today? I think it will be with the devotional book. As I quietly read about the experiences and desires of fellow believers I find both gratitude and longing welling up within me. I take some time to thank God, even for the suffering that others have gone through, so that I might learn and be encouraged. Tears of repentance begin to flow and as no one is there to see or be embarrassed I let them come. I am trying to learn in these precious times to simply go with the flow of the Holy Spirit.

7.25 a.m.   My thoughts are wandering a bit and some distractions are coming in so I change my position and move into the next phase. I used to worry about this aspect of prayer but others who know better than me assure me that it is all part of the package. Usually for me it is the signal to read the scriptures. I pick up my treasured 'One Year Bible'. Having found today's reading I go through another one of my little rituals. Before reading I thank the Lord for all those who have been used by Him to bring me this precious book. I then ask the Holy Spirit to speak directly to me from the word of God. Nothing jumps out of the page at me today but I feel I am being washed inside.

7.35 a.m.   I start to do what most call prayer but I know that I have been 'praying' in all the previous activities. I am into what I call prayer-jogging. In other words I take a portion of scripture and pray it through line by line into my situation. I am using Jabez's prayer (1 Chronicles 4). So I begin to call on the God of Israel. I am glad I am up the garden where no one can hear me! I find the Holy Spirit leading me into prayer themes that don't quite fit in with my theology. I now find myself in tears again praying for the salvation of Israel! Now I feel myself moving up a gear in prayer as I ask for God's blessing on my family. What a privilege to stand in the presence of God and bring my wife and children to Him. Next come the folk that God has given me particular pastoral responsibility for. As I begin to mention them and their children to God I am learning how to know when to stop and home in on a particular situation. So I jog my way through the rest of the prayer.

8.00 a.m.   I've finished my 'Jogging' for today. Having walked about for a while it is time to sit down and have a 'selah'. I usually take communion to finish off with. I will often use parts of the Anglican prayer book, as by faith I eat His 'body' and drink His 'blood'. Again I find myself centred on Christ. It is time to make a good confession using a scripture verse that declares my place in Christ.

8.15 a.m.   Time to say Amen. Time for another cup of black coffee. I get dressed and showered. So many things to do. So many people to see. O Lord, help me to keep listening to you!

84

Postscript

Imagine for a moment that the Queen of England or another head of state personally gave to you a special pass. This pass would enable you to have an audience with them at any time of the day or night. Furthermore they had informed you that they would be completely interested in you and your circumstances during such an audience. You were told that you could be as open with them as you liked and all their resources would be available to you if you were ever in real need or trouble.

In your excitement about this you tell friends and neighbours and regularly refer to your special privilege. One day someone asks you how many times you have used your pass. How surprised they are when they discover that you rarely enjoy the privilege and position you have been granted.

The point, I trust, is obvious. God the Father has given to us, through Jesus, the right to come into His presence anytime. He waits to listen to us, speak to us, and to make Himself available to us. All of this can be regularly enjoyed or neglected. The choice is ours.

Some years ago in our Fellowship we sought the Lord for a word for the New Year. We simply received 'Do It'. The devotional life and the contents of this book can be read, discussed, even made into talks and we can still remain without a consistent time spent with God. We must 'Do It'.

Luke, in his opening chapter of the Acts of the Apostles, states how he previously wrote of all that Jesus began to do and to teach. Jesus did not see teaching as mere theorising. Teaching was given to affect lives. His teaching had to be translated into action. The devotional life must be happening regularly with us. It must grow in our lives, never decline. If we are to know God, be content in our lives and ministries, and be continually fresh in our experience then we must 'do it'.

After Adam and Eve had sinned in the Garden of Eden they tried to hide themselves from the presence of God. The Lord God came to have fellowship with them and called out 'where are you?' (Genesis 3:9). It is my firm conviction that this same question is still being asked by God of us. The reason for this is not because we are hiding through sin but because we do not regularly, and extendedly have fellowship with Him. Let us metaphorically speaking remove the question from our Lord's lips by renewing our desire and determination to spend time with Him.

Do it now.

In your presence, I am content
In your presence, I am content,
In your presence there is light,
Expressions of your life,
Revelations of your power and might,
In your presence I can bring,
My love song offering,
I'm in the presence of my King.*

---

* © Copyright 1986/87 Lifestyle Ministries/Word Music (UK).
Used by permission.